MW00414222

A PITY PARTY
IS STILL A PARTY

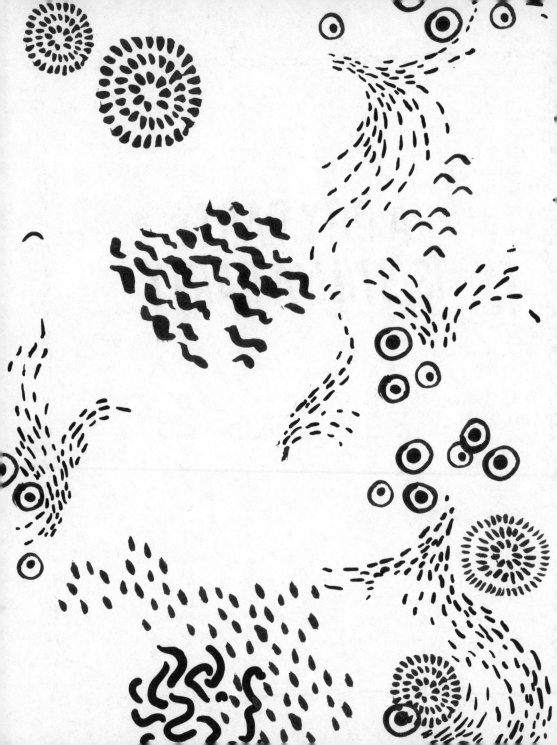

A PITY PARTY
IS STILL A PARTY

A FEEL-GOOD GUIDE TO FEELING BAD

WRITTEN & ILLUSTRATED BY
CHELSEA HARVEY GARNER

HARPER WAVE
An Imprint of HarperCollinsPublishers

A PITY PARTY IS STILL A PARTY. Copyright © 2023 by Chelsea Harvey Garner. All rights reserved. Printed in the United States of America. No part of this book may be used or reproduced in any manner whatsoever without written permission except in the case of brief quotations embodied in critical articles and reviews. For information, address HarperCollins Publishers, 195 Broadway, New York, NY 10007.

HarperCollins books may be purchased for educational, business, or sales promotional use. For information, please email the Special Markets Department at SPsales@harpercollins.com.

FIRST EDITION

Designed by Elina Cohen

Art courtesy of Shutterstock / Valentina_Gurina, Daria Kubrak, inaina, Iliveinoctobe, alonakaporina

Library of Congress Cataloging-in-Publication Data has been applied for.

ISBN 978-0-06-308241-0

23 24 25 26 27 LBC 5 4 3 2 1

FOR THE OUTCASTS, MISFITS, AND ANYONE WHOSE PAIN DOESN'T HAVE A NAME.
MAY WE NEVER STOP SEEKING EACH OTHER.

FOR MY CLIENTS, WHOSE STORIES I SEE THE WORLD THROUGH. YOU'RE HOW I KNOW
THAT A NEW WAY IS POSSIBLE.

AND FOR MY MAMA, WHO TRUSTED ME SO MUCH THAT I COULDN'T HELP BUT TRUST
OTHERS TOO. I'M SO PROUD TO CARRY YOUR TORCH.

CONTENTS

LIVE, LAUGH, LEAVE ME ALONE

WHAT MISERY LOVES

NO UTOPIA

Enjoy your problems.

—Shunryu Suzuki

INTRODUCTION

I WROTE THIS BOOK DURING COVID. NOT THAT I HAVE ANYTHING TO COMPARE IT TO,
but writing a book about pain during a global pandemic felt both more and less difficult
than it might have been otherwise. I thought I had a lot to say about grief in the Before
Times, but boy have I gotten cozier with despair. We all have. We haven't had a choice.
The last few years brought some dark aspects of human psychology to light: in addition
to massive waves of loss, widespread social unrest, and a general sense of terror everywhere, we've also been learning the hard way that we need connection to be well, or
stable, even. During quarantine, rates of depression nearly tripled in the United States.
At first it seemed like technology could keep us connected, but at some point the
group chats silenced and we found ourselves staring at our respective walls, waiting for
something to change. Many of us felt like our mental health was dangling by a thread.
Everyone in the Zoom meeting had that flat, familiar look in their eyes. Small talk went
from uncomfortable to unbearable. Yet as the virus spread and mutated, some people
were unwilling to admit that anything was even happening.

Throughout the pandemic, it seemed like everyone's old boss took to Facebook to
warn that precautions were a way of living in fear. Distant relatives posted vague calls
for unity, hoping others would make sacrifices they weren't willing to make themselves. That guy you went on two dates with claimed the virus didn't even exist until

it arrived in his own neighborhood, family, and finally his own body. Calls for hope started to feel less like attempts to comfort and more like outright refusals to acknowledge any pain that wasn't one's own. One term that emerged during this time is *toxic positivity* (TP), which refers to an ideology promoting an optimistic outlook at all costs. While positivity on its own is great, toxic positivity takes it too far by implying that attitude is the only thing that matters, and that by changing our mindset we can alter or even evade the most painful aspects of existence. This is especially offensive when expressed in the face of tragedy and injustice, as it essentially blames people for their suffering. At its core, toxic positivity is a form of avoidance. One might imagine that a multitiered, worldwide emergency would be enough to get even the most avoidant person to admit that times are tough, but unlike the other form of TP, toxic positivity was not in short supply.

For months, the public discourse kept shifting from strategies for resolving the crisis to debates about whether there actually was one. No proof seemed to be enough. Unless you were a researcher studying self-fulfilling prophecies, it was a great time to uninstall social media. In our isolation, however, most of us developed even more of an addiction to it. As I paced my apartment doom-scrolling and weeping, I became convinced that our collective tendency to look on the bright side isn't just annoying, it's dangerous, and it's partly to blame for the mess we're in now.

Perhaps one genuinely positive outcome of the pandemic was the way it gave people permission to feel bad publicly without explaining why. Bosses became more lax about deadlines, friends stopped asking why we were wearing the same outfit for days, strangers saw us stifling tears and nodded in camaraderie. No one needed to justify why they felt and looked awful because everyone assumed this was the hardest thing any of us had been through. And while this shift was vital, it was also overdue. Every problem COVID created already existed for someone. Many of us had been hurting that much or worse our whole lives, but when our pain couldn't be explained by a pandemic, we were expected to keep it to ourselves.

Not only did recent years bring an increase in permission to feel, they brought an increase in discussions about mental health. As rates of mental illness soared, people started sharing what they were learning in therapy, even encouraging others to get a therapist. As much as I've loved to see it, I think it's important to remember that therapists aren't miracle workers. I'm a therapist, and I'm also just a person. Like you, I have insecurities and blind spots. Like you, I stress-baked a cake yesterday and ate the whole thing with my hands. Throughout the pandemic, I struggled alongside my clients and colleagues to remain stable in the wake of near-constant crises. And while I believe in the power of therapy, I don't think it's enough to solve the current mental health epidemic. There's a very real limit to what we therapists can do to help our clients when the culture itself is antagonistic to many of their basic needs.

At the end of the day, therapists are in the same mess as everyone else. Therapy has an important role to play in shifting the cultural tide, but what we really need is to fundamentally alter the way we coexist. We need to create a society where people help each other before things get dire. To do this, we'll have to lean further into the embarrassing art of exposing ourselves. Not in a gross way, don't be weird. We need to share our woes when they're major and when they're minor. Yes, get a therapist, but also get better at being honest with the people in your life about how you're doing. Don't just talk about your feelings once they've passed, show them in real time. Cry at work. Thank others when they do the same. Go out of your way to show up for the people in your life. Get out of bed at 2:00 a.m. and drive to your friend's house if that's what would help. Let them snot on your sweater, then play their favorite song and take them to get French fries. In order to build a future where mental health is even possible, we'll have to remember how to count on each other. This will mean being witnessed at our worst. Things might get weirder before they get normal-er, and we're going to have to see each other through those hard times.

You won't get quick or easy answers here. I don't think you're going to get them elsewhere either, and, ultimately, they're not what we need. We need to ask hard questions. We need to do the slow work of remembering how to feel, but we don't have to do it alone and it doesn't have to be miserable. Bonding at rock bottom can be empowering, relieving, and, dare I say, fun. In doing so, we are reminded that being a person, even in the darkest of days, is a pretty good gig. As I write this, I'm still alive. If you're reading it, so are you. I think that's cause for celebration. And while I'm sad that we can't celebrate together today, I know there will be a time when we can. We will be together again. We'll dance together. We'll laugh and cry together, and if I have my way, we'll do them all at once.

WHO THIS BOOK IS FOR

This book is for those who have been told to cheer up, who can't pretend to feel fine when they're not, who cry while reading the news, and who don't know where their grief ends and the world's begins. It's for people who are lonely. It's for those who are afraid to ask for help, who are recovering from a life of suffering in silence. It's for people who don't belong to a culture they feel safe in, who didn't get a handbook for life's struggles from family or religion, or who did get a handbook but it sucked. It's for those who come from lost or broken lineages, who are raising children with more compassion than they were raised with and trying to show their elders a better way. It's for people who check in on those who are suffering even when they themselves are heartbroken and grief-stricken, people who identify as highly sensitive, who don't want to give up on humanity. It's for the witches and the rogue healers. It's for the therapists, social workers, and the night-shift nurses bringing my father fresh water, and anyone trying to hold the hurting together. This book is for people who are tired.

What you take from the ideas outlined here will be specific to your identity and history, just as what I've written was informed by mine.

WHO THIS BOOK IS BY

I'm Chelsea. I'm a psychotherapist, writer, and founding director of Big Feels Lab: a nonprofit promoting collective mental health. My pronouns are she/her. I'm a deep thinker and deep feeler. Friends describe me as intense, fun, and, frankly, not very chill. I'm one of those people who not only dislikes small talk but finds it confusing and anxiety-producing. Before becoming a therapist, I was an enthusiastic therapy client. I'd show up each week, genuinely pumped to process whatever I was grappling with. I'd been going for years before I realized that other people don't think therapy is fun. Like, someone is just going to listen to me? And help me sort through my most unfiltered thoughts and feelings?? How is that not a good time?!? To each their own, I guess.

For as long as I can remember, I've been fascinated by emotions. I love psychology, philosophy, and sociology because I'm driven to understand how life feels to those whose experience differs from mine. I wasn't necessarily a bookish kid (more into making potions and interviewing neighbors about the mystery of the missing stray cat), but I did find myself scribbling stories, poems, essays, and lyrics onto scraps of paper wherever I went. I've always used art to turn the world sideways and see it anew. I've written a lot of books already (The Beginner's Guide to Potions, Missing Cat Chronicles) but this is the first one to be published, so I'm pretty stoked you're here.

For the personality-type people, I'm an Enneagram 8 wing 7, ENFJ-A, Explorer. Taurus sun, Libra rising, Virgo moon. I was born in Texas and raised in Nebraska. I'm an only child and was adopted by my grandmother, whom you'll hear more about soon. I'm a feminist (because I believe men are as capable of kindness as everyone else), poet (though I think most poetry is bad), musician and music freak (constantly singing in places where that's discouraged), and lifelong dancer (though for me, dance is less about choreography and more about release). I'm obsessed with wild animals and insects and the many forms a body can take.

I draw from paganism (read: witchcraft) and Buddhism in my spiritual practice and am also influenced by existentialism and the burgeoning field of somatics. I was raised in a community of punk rock weirdos, so the part of me that still wants to impress hipsters by being ambiguous and ironic is at odds with the super-sincere part of me that wants to write love poems to flowers. If you pay attention, you can see that tension play out on these pages. Above all, I believe in connection. I believe in magic and the dignity of what we can't understand. I believe most of us are doing our best and that it's good that we're alive. Even now, right in the mess of it, even still.

HOW TO READ THIS BOOK

I was once at a party in a California mansion with a bunch of half-naked life coaches. While wandering through the house trying to avoid another three-minute hug, I found a book on a coffee table and started thumbing through it. Soon, two unnecessarily hot women rushed over to inform me I was reading the book the wrong way. Apparently, the author was present and had expressly stated in the book's intro that it was not to be read in a distracting environment. I opened to the beginning and, sure enough, there was a section forbidding readers from consuming the text in an unfocused manner. Intrigued, I had these helpful guests lead me to the esteemed author, who turned out to be (you guessed it) an old guy with a ponytail. I tried to engage him about the vision of his work, but he mostly sat smiling while another man I was pretty sure was Sting treated us to an impromptu didgeridoo performance. It was not Sting.

I am not the ponytail guy. I want you to read this book in whatever way is most convenient. Thumb through it at a party, pretend to read it on the train so the person next to you stops (or starts) talking. My hope is that you'll use what you find here to move further into your life, rather than retreating from it. Although if you need to retreat for a while, I'm happy to join you there as well.

Everything in this book is an invitation. Some of what's written is meant to push you outside your comfort zone, but the challenge should be rewarding and exciting, not torturous or terrifying. Only you will know where that line is, and it may change from day to day. That's okay. You get to decide. Just because I work in mental health doesn't mean I know what's best for you. We are the experts on ourselves, and we have the right to pick and choose what healing practices work for us. So while I hope you'll find what's written herein helpful, I trust that you'll know if something isn't a fit. If that's the case, I invite you to disregard that section.

Logistically, the book is organized into essays, activities, and science-y lists. I know how tired our brains are, so I tried to break ideas into bite-size chunks. In terms of activities, some are designed to be practiced alone, and some require a group. The activities are marked with an asterisk in the Table of Contents, so if you want to skip straight to those, you can find them more easily. There are also journal prompts throughout. You can obviously write on your phone, but there are mental health benefits to the old-fashioned method of writing stuff on paper, so you may want to think about getting a journal if you don't already have one.

CAN YOU PITY PARTY TOO HARD?

I know what some of you are thinking, Can't you take the whole pity partying thing too far? Yes, yes, you can. Of course! Anything can be taken too far. But you can also not pity party hard enough, and that's what most of us are currently doing, so.

Pity partying is an art. Skill is required to do it well. There are a few key warning signs that will tell you when you're taking it too far, each of which we'll cover in greater depth farther into the book. For now, just keep an eye out for these things.

Putting Things Off. Pity partying is not about doing nothing about our problems. It's about getting in touch with what we're feeling so we can make better choices. If you notice that you're putting off important decisions for more than a few days, that might be a sign that your party is headed the wrong direction.

Apathy. Pity partying is about learning to work with our sadness. The goal is not to become cynical, apathetic, or hopeless. Gloria Steinem once described the difference between sadness and depression this way: "In depression, nothing matters. In sadness, everything matters." If we start to notice that events which would normally spark emotion for us now leave us feeling nothing, this could be cause for concern.

Isolation. This is the one to really watch for. We all want to be alone sometimes, and there's nothing wrong with that in doses. But if we start isolating in ways that are atypical for us, or stop sharing important information with the people we're closest to, we should reach out to a therapist.

In addition to isolating behavior, look out for isolating thoughts. These sound like: No one understands me, and nobody else has this problem. No matter what you're feeling, someone else has felt it, too. We want our pain to link us up with others, not position us farther apart.

Some signs that you're pity partying *well* include:

◦ experiencing a deeper sense of connection

◦ feeling more empathy for yourself and others

◦ having greater clarity around your thoughts and feelings

◦ seeing the world as more heartbreaking and beautiful

◦ practicing new rituals for moving through emotions

◦ generally getting cooler and weirder

MEET THE PHONE FAIRY

I won't lie, I'm totally addicted to my phone. I am decidedly pro-tech, and I believe the internet has the power to radically alter our world for good. THAT SAID, I can't deny the negative effects of tech on our mental health. Smartphones and most of the apps on them are designed to be addictive, and have basically hacked our poor little brains. They promote distraction and, in the day of scary news cycles, anxiety.

Our dependence on technology also has an impact on our social skills. Older generations are now accusing younger ones of having forgotten how to have a conversation, and while I think that argument might be a little simplistic, there's some truth to it. Our phones allow for certain forms of communication, but there's no replacement for in-person bonding. I don't think the problem is that we've forgotten how to talk (humans have never been great at that), but more so that we've forgotten how to be present. This tendency toward dissociation isn't great for personal or collective health.

When we're trying to connect deeply with others or ourselves, we need to bring our full attention to what we're doing. We need to focus on our senses of sight, sound, taste, touch, smell. Phones make this difficult. There is always another meme, article, or person to swipe on. For this reason, I've invited the Phone Fairy to help us to put these magical devices down. Whenever it's especially important that we be present, the Phone Fairy will be there with a gentle reminder. Think of her like the mama phone who's coming to have her own party with her babies. The Phone Fairy recommends buying a basket (thrift stores have tons of them), decorating it, and leaving it by the door when you host events or practice these activities yourself. Maybe you can even invest in a couple extra chargers for different phone types so everyone can leave with a fully charged device!

DESPAIR, BUT MAKE IT FASHION

RETHINKING MENTAL HEALTH

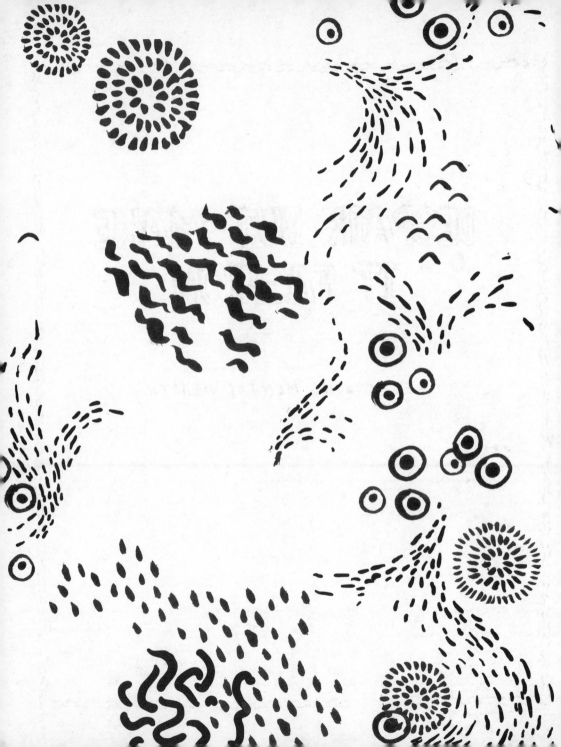

THE CRY BABY CREED

♥ Let our hearts break. Get softer, not harder. (Most important.)

♥ Let our feelings show. Pay more than lip service to the idea that pain is real.

♥ Take opportunities to stop what we're doing and lie down in the grass.

♥ Be as close to the bodies of others as is mutually beneficial.

♥ Bring people the food they love most.

♥ Offer to go with others where they're afraid to go alone.

♥ 'Fess up to our fears and the strange things they make us say and do.

♥ Come out of our hiding places. Or, invite others into them to listen to music or take a nap.

♥ Remember that everyone believes what they do because they think it will protect them and the people they love.

♥ Take off our armor as soon as we can. (And trying to be right is armor.)

SOB STORY

WHEN I WAS TEN, I TOLD MY GRANDMA I WANTED TO DIE. WHILE PERHAPS A BIT dramatic (theater kid), I remember feeling like I meant it. My parents had been in and out of my life, struggling with addiction. The other kids in my neighborhood were bullying me relentlessly after their parents found out about my family's history. I felt like agony was emanating from me, a bat signal no one answered. When the ridicule got extreme, the school called my grandma and me in for a chat. Everyone's advice was the same: don't let the bullies see that you're hurting. If you do, they will have won. It took my well-meaning teachers by surprise when I asked: But if I'm already hurting, what good will hiding it do? Isn't feeling so ashamed that I only cry alone even worse? My grandmother, a fierce woman with a perpetually broken heart, beamed at me with pride, and I've been crying in public ever since.

As rough as aspects of my childhood were, I feel fortunate to have landed in the care of a person who understood that feelings are healthy. My grandma, who became mama to me, never told me not to cry. She helped me see that the feelings I thought were too big to feel were just too big to feel alone. Her affection and even her company weren't contingent on my emotional state. Whatever mood arose, she tried to find a way for us to explore it together. When I had panic attacks at school, she picked me up for special lunches. When my mom overdosed and went back to prison, she encouraged me to write about my feelings, then scratched my back as I read my bad poetry aloud. If I wanted to be alone, she respected that. She drank coffee nearby as I blasted the *Titanic* soundtrack, performing sad operas to my reflection in the mirror.

Years later, when her death threw me face-first into the feeling I feared most, I trusted I could handle it. Not saying it was easy, or that I didn't lie prostrate in the hallway of my university on several occasions, but I had some deep faith I'd be okay. I knew I could recover, so I felt free to fall apart. Ironically, this permission to feel bad made me feel better, and I was surprised to find a strange, primal pleasure in the rituals of grief. There was something affirming about loving someone so much that their death ravaged me. The grief was a testament to the love, and I felt grateful I knew how to feel both. So while I wouldn't jump at the chance to go through it again, loss did help me learn that any feeling we lean into is easier to manage.

Predictably, the kids who bullied me in childhood want to be friends now. (Fuck you, Jamie Cruise.) Looking back, I see that their cruelty was as much confusion as disapproval. Most of them had been made to feel ashamed when they expressed vulnerability. They'd been told to suck it up by their parents who'd been told to suck it up by their parents. Because I didn't see them expressing their emotions, I assumed I was the only one hurting as much as I was. Now I know many of them were hurting, too. I don't blame anyone from back then for hiding how they felt. We all have reason to fear opening up. But whether we embrace tough feelings or not, life is hard. I'm convinced that everyone's life sounds like a sob story if you listen long enough.

For this reason, I raise an eyebrow whenever I see someone sporting Good Vibes Only gear. Sure, life is beautiful, but good vibes *only*? In this economy? Demanding good vibes only from ourselves is like demanding Good Smells Only from our bodies. It just doesn't work that way. To be alive is to experience a smorgasbord of vibes every day, starting on day one. If you've ever witnessed a birth, you know what I mean. In the best of conditions, life gets off to a weird start. Everyone's crying, each for different reasons. If birth were a party and your friend got there first, they'd tell you not to come. Alas, birth was the first party any of us attended. A bloody, spectacular party, and we were once the life of it. We shot out of that slippery flesh canal screaming and crying. Our wailing made bystanders cover their ears, but we were unconcerned, so complete was our faith that our bad vibes mattered.

Birth involves just about every emotion smashed together in a seemingly random order, and really, that's a pretty accurate preview of what's to come. As adults, we may feel boredom and relief, elation and terror, sometimes in the span of a minute. As babies, we went from giggling to weeping without even thinking to apologize for the shifts. But somewhere along the way, Jamie Cruise or someone like her told us that screaming every time we feel bad is "rude" and "disruptive" and "scaring the customers." The more we concealed our struggles, the more we started to wonder if everyone else was pretending, too, or if they'd learned something we hadn't.

Let's get one thing straight: pain is part of the human experience. In the words of R.E.M., everybody hurts. Pain is not a sign of failure, weakness, or spiritual disfavor. Likewise, happiness is not a reward. It's not proof that you know some ancient secret or have made good choices. It's not necessarily even evidence of mental health. Every feeling has a function. A healthy, fulfilling life involves a wide range of emotions. Rather than trying to exist in a state of perpetual calm, we're better off accepting that we're going to experience a lot of emotions in life, some of which will suck. This attitude makes us more resilient. Our efforts to avoid feeling bad often make us feel worse and amplify the emotion we're trying to avoid. When avoidance is our default strategy, we also fail to learn the skills to manage stress well. We become fragile. Basically, the whole thing backfires.

A more effective attitude is seeing suffering as a part of life. The Buddha put it something like: pain is inevitable, but suffering is optional. I'm not convinced that suffering is optional, but regardless, I think his point is that resisting a feeling makes it worse. Feelings are our internal weather; they naturally come and go. If we learn to see them less as good or bad and more as ever-shifting responses to our inner and outer environment, we'll develop a more realistic view of wellness. None of this means we should turn a blind eye toward abuse or injustice, of course. Suffering may be intrinsic to life, but oppression doesn't have to be. When we're being mistreated, reflection is not the answer. Turning inward is important, but so is turning outward and saying no, that's not okay. The two are not mutually exclusive.

Not only does embracing our emotions make them more bearable, it helps us savor life more fully. The greater the variety of feelings we can welcome, the greater the likelihood that any given moment will be enjoyable. We don't have to stop at tolerating our experience. Rather than wishing bad feelings away, we can learn to explore them, celebrate them even. The key is curiosity. We must become fascinated by our experience, regardless of its quality. When we're sad, we can throw our sadness a party. We can build an altar to our agony and decorate it with objects that are the color of how we feel. We can create rituals of sadness, like watching sad movies or taking a walk in the woods. We can sing songs to our sadness and celebrate its particularity. The goal is not to fall in love with our sorrow, but to fall so in love with ourselves that we don't prefer our joy over any other feeling. A bonus of this approach is that it drives haters crazy. Can you imagine? Your enemy stumbles upon you arranging items on your agony altar. (Which you'll learn how to make soon.) Confusing, cool, and a little bit creepy. It's perfect.

THE STRUGGLE IS REAL

BEFORE WE GO ANY FURTHER, LET'S DO A CHECK-IN. HOW'S EVERYBODY FEELING out there?!

These days, you don't have to be a therapist to sense that the mood is grim. Generally speaking, people aren't doing so hot. Injustice appears to be everywhere, the earth is trying to break up with us, and it turns out that staring into tiny doom screens all day isn't great for morale. We feel like we could sleep forever, but we also can't sit still. To put it simply, the struggle is real. Thankfully, the conversations we're having about individual wellness and community care are shifting. Our collective standards have gone up so much so fast that any movie made before the year 2000 now seems cruel and absurd. And while there's a ton of work left to do, we appear to have the means and motivation to do it, with tools that past generations could only dream of. So why do we still feel so bad?

For starters, mental health is an extraordinarily complex issue. Even defining it is difficult: sadness and depression are not the same, but they're connected. Mental health is impacted by genetics, and yet our environment and experience greatly influence how those genes are expressed. There is no single factor that causes mental illness and no single factor that can cure it. This makes it extremely difficult to know if our mental health is actually getting worse, or if our understanding of it is expanding, or if our tools of measuring it are growing, or if all of these things, or something else,

is true. One thing we do know is that the social conditions we live in broadly affect our health, as do the quality of our relationships. What this means is that to change the way we feel, we also must change how we interact with each other.

These days, we hear the word "unprecedented" a lot. In some ways, we are living in a unique time with unique problems. In other ways, we're not. Sorrow is timeless. It's the little black dress of emotion. Violence is certainly not new, and data actually suggests that it has consistently declined over time, although such a broad claim is tough to prove. Yet in the Era of the Endless Scroll, that's difficult to believe. Our news feeds are blasting the most horrendous things humans are doing and have ever done into our brains nonstop, making it easy for any sensitive person to come to the conclusion that things are worse than they've ever been. And while we'll likely never know if that's true, what we can be sure of is that people today are more aware of the violence taking place, which in itself has an effect on our outlook. Consistent intake of negative news has been linked with anxiety, depression, and PTSD symptoms. Studies found that individuals exposed to extensive media coverage of the Boston Marathon bombings experienced more acute distress than those who were actually at or near the event. Regardless of whether the past was worse, people used to be much more ignorant, and you know what they say about that.

THE AGE OF TMI

Over the last several decades, technological advances have completely transformed the human experience. In 2017, researchers estimated that the average person took in about 74 GB of data a day. That's the equivalent of about fifteen thousand songs, sixteen movies, or 26 million text messages. Way, way more than our ancestors used to get.

For perspective, a highly educated person who lived five hundred years ago would likely have consumed 74 GB of data in their lifetime. While this does imply that the average person living today is more knowledgeable than most humans who've ever lived, knowledge isn't always power. Because our brains haven't evolved to take in this much information, a modern data diet can be extremely disorienting.

Our nervous systems are wired to continuously scan our environment for threats. When we sense danger, our sympathetic nervous system gets activated and responds in ways that help us survive. When the threat has passed, we flip back into a parasympathetic state. Because life is more complicated these days, it's harder to tell what is or isn't a threat. Is a news alert about a mass shooting in the next state over a threat? How about a spreadsheet listing daily COVID deaths? Or your ex posting a selfie with his beautiful new partner? Our bodies don't know and neither do we. The solution, of course, is not to throw our phones into the ocean. (Although, dear reader, I think about it every day.) Sticking our heads in the proverbial sand will only prolong the issues we've already been ignoring for millennia. The trick is figuring out how to stay informed enough to make changes without feeling so overwhelmed that we can't function.

Taking in this much stimulus means sorting through complex, divergent perspectives at a near-constant rate. That's a physically exhausting task. The brain isn't some magical machine that hovers above our bodies, it's an organ. Sometimes it stops working, the same way our hands cramp up after a day of writing. (As a totally hypothetical example.) While it makes up just 2 percent of our body mass, the brain uses about 20 percent of the calories we consume. Even at rest, the human brain burns more fuel than a thigh does while running a marathon. Like every other part of our bodies, tired brains don't work as well. And when we're mentally depleted, one of the first things to go is nuance.

When we're stressed, our thoughts become more simplistic. Good, bad. Danger, opportunity. All, nothing. We're not trying to write poetry in a crisis, we're just trying to get through it. Subtlety isn't as important when we're in survival mode. Reality, however, is full of complexities. Paradoxes. Seeming contradictions. The more exhausted our brains are, the more we miss these gray areas. As you might be able to guess, this isn't great for decision-making. Which, by the way, we do more of than our ancestors did as well. Considering all of this, it's unsurprising that *burnout* is a very real problem of our era and has been linked to multiple mental health issues. As troubling as that is, the impact it has on our social behavior may be even more concerning.

Research has found that burnout and its companion, *compassion fatigue* (a form of emotional exhaustion experienced by those in helping roles), have been linked to cynicism and lack of impulse control. This can result in a general feeling of apathy and lack of concern for others, even in instances when one would normally care. Burnout increases the likelihood that we'll make snap judgments about others or simply ignore how they're feeling. Combine this with the fact that technology exposes us to endless requests for assistance, often from people whose needs and lifestyles we don't understand, and we're really off to the races. As our level of awareness grows and our ability to cope shrinks, the chronic overwhelm of our nervous systems becomes a vicious cycle.

A ZOOM OF ONE'S OWN

We're exhausted, we're grouchy, and we miss our ignorance. But the fun doesn't stop there, folks. People living today are also increasingly disconnected from each other. Humans are social creatures. At every stage of life, we need each other both to survive and to thrive. The longest-running study on human health and happiness ever conducted found that no factor played quite as central a role as the quality of our relationships. Namely, the feeling that we had at least one person in life we can really count on. Capitalism has tried hard to make us forget this. Under capitalism, disconnection is a good thing. The more detached people are from each other, the more stuff they have to buy. If people remember how to depend on one another (read: to share), there won't be as many products to sell us.

While there are some values associated with capitalism, like autonomy and choice, that have mental health benefits, much of its impact has been disastrous for global well-being. For one, our obsession with freedom has significantly impacted the structure of our communities. In the United States, people tend to reflexively reject any suggestion that requires us to be more reliant on others. Because of the value that capitalism places on independence, recent generations have grown up being told to be as needless as possible and to count on only ourselves. The impact this has on our mental health can't be overstated. Loneliness is a significant predictor of mental illness, as well as suicidal ideation and self-harming behaviors. Just expressing difficult feelings to others reduces their intensity, but since we live in a culture that makes us feel ashamed to reach out, we're less likely to seek that support.

Humans are wired to regulate our emotions best together. When we process and soothe our emotions through connection, that's called co-regulation. Self-regulation is important, but it's actually possible only after learning to soothe ourselves alongside another person. Ideally, we grew up with at least one supportive adult who modeled healthy emotion regulation. Even if that was the case, we manage our emotions best at any age when in the presence of other supportive people. As constant news cycles keep us feeling stressed and powerless, our lack of connection reduces our capacity to return to an emotionally regulated state. So while it's miraculous that we can get so many needs met through these pocket computers, it will never quite do the trick.

Technology use has also been linked to dissociation, which is a psychological state in which one feels disconnected from their own body and identity. While dissociation can be a coping mechanism under dire circumstances, it's also correlated to serious mental health issues. For many of us, a sedentary lifestyle exaggerates the feeling of being a floating head with a body attached, and more and more of our jobs have us sitting in one place all day. Our lack of regular movement also keeps us from releasing energy stored in the body during times of stress, and that chemical buildup can contribute to anxiety, depression, and chronic pain. But if we can agree that we've become detached from our bodies, one could argue we're even more detached from the earth.

Our bodies are part of the earth. That's not a metaphor or a poetic sentiment, it's a simple fact. These days, it feels like the earth is just a place we park our bodies so we can text. Our lack of respect for the sophistication of our own physicality is evident in our lack of respect for the living earth around us, and the many life-forms that our habits have obliterated. From a mental health perspective, dissociation from ourselves and the earth have a similarly alienating effect, leaving us feeling like we don't belong in our bodies or the ecosystems that we're born braided into. The mental health benefits of time spent in nature are widely documented and understood, but it goes beyond the data. Nature moves in cycles and phases, while our current way of life encourages a static, constant state of production. Nature's abundance exists by way of both on and off seasons, as well as a balance between species. Humans prefer to ignore this in favor of nonstop, infinite demands. The more we attune to our place in nature, the more we can remember and embrace healthy fluctuations and limitations within ourselves.

In our divergence from the ways of the past, we've also lost our sense of ceremony. In times of great stress, ritual has been shown to dramatically improve our ability to cope with change and tolerate uncertainty. Ritual provides a source of meaning-making, social bonding, and emotional catharsis. As many of us are either leaving formal religion or seeking a new belief system, we may feel unsure what ritual could do for us. Even those who maintain a personal connection to tradition often lack a community to practice with. Whatever the case may be, our collective lack of ritual makes it harder for our societies to move through these massive waves of upheaval with grace.

NOW YOU FEEL WORSE

Look, I know it seems like the world is falling apart, or like a veneer has been stripped and we're taking a long, hard look at what was festering underneath it. One could liken being alive today to having surgery done without anesthesia. It's painful. We're currently being forced to reconsider everything we thought we knew. Even if we try to tune the world out, we're affected by it because we're a part of the world.

thanks
a lot

Nothing happens in a vacuum. And while we're pretty sure we can't continue with business as usual, we don't necessarily know what to do instead. Every question we ask seems to reveal another question. Getting to a new set of answers is going to ask each of us to be brave.

It makes sense that we all feel a little (or a lot) weird. But remember: like everything, this is a phase. No phase lasts forever. There's an immense amount of change taking place and a lot of death, it's true. If we want the future to be any better than the past, we'll have to remember how to mourn what's gone. We'll have to take stock of what we've learned and try to put it to use. Amid all the endings, new beginnings are coming. We can't know what the future will look like. If we can lean into the mystery of that, we have a chance to make the years to come much gentler and more caring. With a bit more courage and a lot more crying, we may be able to make the next era truly unprecedented.

THINKING STRAIGHT

Our feelings are our most genuine paths to
knowledge.

—Audre Lorde

MY GRANDMA HAD A DIFFICULT LIFE. I GREW UP HEARING SNIPPETS ABOUT HER
childhood, tales she'd distilled to medicinal doses during decades of therapy. I'd heard
about how she'd watched her father burn in a fire that later took his life, how she'd
gotten pregnant at fifteen and had four kids by twenty, how my grandpa beat her and
left her for the nanny. I'd learned about her years spent in the grip of addiction, and
how she'd gotten sober through AA and become a mentor to others. I was hungry for
these stories, which occasionally made her tear up as she told them. I'd listen and think
about how smart and tough she'd had to be to survive all of this. Each year I'd beg for
more gruesome details, trying to prove I was mature enough to handle them. When
she thought I was too young for certain parts, she'd pat me on the back and give me
the moral, which was usually some version of "trust how you feel."

As one of the first female brakemen for the railroad, she'd had to learn to fit into
hyper-masculine settings often. Her temperament was naturally sweet, but she could
also be brash. She refused to let the men around her imply that her emotionality was
weakness. She saw numbing out as the real act of cowardice. I wasn't alive to hear these
colleagues ridicule her for being too sensitive, but I could sense the imprint their accusations had left in her. She was always ready to defend her feelings and the feelings of

others. When she told her story or talked about her perspective, she did so with a hard-won dignity. She insisted on being taken seriously even while trembling, and when men mocked her for this, she happily cut them down to size (which was very fun to watch).

She resisted the anti-emotionality that trails so many survivors, threatening to undermine not just accounts of their history but their credibility as a person if they dare to show one bit of feeling. The older I get, the more I value her stories and the way she told them. Like folklore, they populate my psyche with triumphs of empathy and a rugged protection of tenderness. Like most women, I later came to experience these same accusations of being too sensitive myself. Many times, in personal and professional settings, I've been asked not to let my feelings get "in the way" and to try to "think straight."

The more I learn about mental health, the more ridiculous this advice sounds. Humans are profoundly emotional creatures, and this isn't necessarily at odds with our ability to reason. The sentiment of anti-emotionality that permeates our culture is rooted in a misunderstanding, an assumption that we have logical thoughts and illogical feelings. This is far from the case, yet this misconception even pervades the field of psychology, where many traditional models of treatment train therapists to regard strong emotions as a red flag. While old-school therapists likely wouldn't state a disdain for emotion directly, much of the attitude they've been encouraged to embody is one of stoicism, placidity, and calm-at-all-costs. The example that this demeanor provides to therapy clients inadvertently reinforces the idea that mental health is a matter of toning down our emotions so that thoughts alone can guide us. For those whose emotions are the key to their healing, this method can both delay this process and perpetuate shame. On a social level, the fallout can be even worse.

Many of my clients come to me having already internalized the assumption that their feelings are the problem. They don't say this explicitly, but in so many words:

"If I wasn't so sad, I could get back to work."

"I'm furious with my boyfriend, but I have no reason to be."

"I'm always overreacting. I don't know why I'm so sensitive."

It seems that many assume the goal of therapy is to eliminate bad or strong feelings in general. This tracks with the Western model of medicine, where the symptoms of a condition are to be masked without much curiosity about their cause. But feelings aren't symptoms of ill health. They aren't even a divergence from the norm the way a fever or a headache would be—they *are* the norm. Research has shown that humans are feeling at least one emotion roughly 90 percent of the time. Emotional states are not limited to the rising and falling of intense, negative feelings, as the colloquial understanding implies. They're a near-constant feature of the human experience. So if we believe that feelings in and of themselves cloud our judgment, we should be prepared to be in a cloudy state most of our lives.

Because emotions are a primary source of information for humans, trying to ignore them really just results in our turning the volume down on our experience in general. Don't get me wrong; I understand why we want to do this. The world is loud, and so are our reactions to it. Much of the time, I don't want to feel my feelings either. Since we're taught that emotions are irrational, untrustworthy, and generally a sign of weakness, we think we're doing right by ourselves when we overlook how we feel. We think that by dismissing the knot in our stomach, we're being mature. We think that by focusing exclusively on logic, we'll make better choices. But really, we need access to our feelings to make good decisions. Our feelings, as much as our thoughts, help us determine what matters as well as what's right and wrong for us. Much of the work of therapy lies in helping clients return to emotions they've been cut off from. In doing so, people who've felt stuck on a choice, sometimes for decades, may instantly know what to do. Whether it's a woman who's denied that her marriage is abusive, someone who chose a profession they're not suited for, or a parent whose gay child has them feeling conflicted about their beliefs, feelings are often the key to clarity.

The idea that it's even possible to separate feelings from thoughts is half-baked. Ideas and emotions are intertwined. They inform and reinforce each other. The systems of thinking and feeling work together to make sense of our endlessly shifting environment. Both take place in our bodies. They're physiological events. And while we may think of thoughts as more abstract or ephemeral, they actually tend to arise in response to emotion. They are each bound by our biology and therefore our limited perspective. Sure, emotions can lead us astray at times, but thoughts are just as likely to be biased or simply random. Have you ever sat and just observed your train of thought? If you have, then you know how incoherent thoughts can be.

The belief that a person is either being logical or emotional is scientifically baseless, but that's not really my problem with it. The social implications of this idea are dangerous. When we conflate emotional expression with an absence of rational thought, we assume that anyone who's openly hurting is being unreasonable. This means that we feel free to discredit the point of view of those who are most overtly struggling, a strategy we see playing out far too often on the political stage. Just because someone is grieving or starving or terrified doesn't mean that they're not making perfect sense. There are situations in which intense emotions like despair or rage are the most reasonable response.

In order to be truly reasonable, we need access to both our thoughts and feelings. When we don't trust our emotions, it becomes difficult to navigate our experience. We may endlessly try to weigh pros and cons without an inner compass telling us which way to go. We start to regard each other's vulnerability with skepticism and lack the empathy needed to connect well. Instead of saying "wait until you're thinking straight" we could try saying "wait until you understand your thoughts and feelings." That's actually good advice. It does mean, however, that we'll have to get better at feeling things.

REPRESSION CONFESSIONS

The avoidance of pain, physical or psychic, is
a dangerous mechanism, which can cause us to
lose touch not just with our painful sensations
but with ourselves.

—Adrienne Rich

REPRESSION MAY BE COMMON, BUT IT'S NOT WITHOUT CONSEQUENCE. IN OUR ATTEMPTS
to repress painful feelings, we inadvertently numb all our emotions and limit our capacity to feel joy and connection. When we're repressed, we feel far away from what's
happening. We feel detached, distracted, and aimless. We struggle to know what we
want or don't want and may lack an overall sense of purpose. This is because emotions
are more than occasional bursts of energy, they are our internal radar. Emotions not
only help us make major decisions, they keep us alive on a daily basis. We evolved to
feel emotions so that we could rapidly and efficiently respond to a variety of cues from
our environment. Emotions allow us to synthesize broad inputs of data and experience
them as one unified impulse. Repression, then, cuts us off from important messages
our body is trying to communicate to us. While it makes sense as a temporary coping
skill under certain dire circumstances, repression is not a pathway to clarity or health.
In fact, it can make us sick.

Because emotions are physical processes, repressing them has a physical effect. In their book *Burnout*, authors Amelia Nagoski and Emily Nagoski discuss the relationship between emotion and chronic fatigue. As it turns out, burnout is caused in large part by the experience of getting "stuck" in an emotion without moving through it fully. Studies have also shown significant links between emotional repression and disease, including an increased risk of developing cancer and greater mortality across demographics.

That said, simply knowing that repression is dangerous doesn't solve the problem. Many have been repressing their whole lives. After decades, repression has likely become a habitual, unconscious pattern. A person may not even realize they're doing it. To others, people who repress may seem healthy and may even be lauded for their calm demeanor. This is because it can be easy to confuse repression with emotional regulation. To quote psychologist Marc Brackett, "Repression is actually a form of regulation," just not a very healthy one. Repression differs from healthy regulation in some important ways. Where repression involves avoiding emotion, regulation involves managing emotion. When we regulate our feelings, we experience them without being overtaken by them.

From the outside, repression and regulation may look the same. But repression usually involves a lack of emotional expression, where regulation may involve a variety of outward expressions. One common misconception is that regulating an emotion means not outwardly showing signs of feeling. In truth, we can effectively regulate our emotions while venting, crying, or exhibiting any other emotional state. Just as someone who appears to be calm may be experiencing profound internal struggle, someone who is showing an intense display of emotionality may still be within the zone of emotional arousal in which they are able to function well, also known as the *window of tolerance*. Within our window of tolerance, emotions may be heightened, but we feel able to cope with them. We're able to identify that we're feeling something, and we understand that it won't last forever. We're able to stay grounded in the present moment by engaging in soothing or cathartic activities. When we're repressing, we may be unaware that we're feeling anything at all. We may feel compelled to engage with distractions before pausing to reflect. We may behave in ways we can't explain or which are concerning to others, like drinking to excess or becoming consumed in an activity for long periods without eating.

I don't say any of this to criticize those who repress. We all do it sometimes. Some of us need to numb out to survive our circumstances. If we have survived or are still living through trauma, we may genuinely not be prepared to deal with our emotions. Coming back to our feelings and growing our window of tolerance can take years of steady healing work. And even when we've gained emotional awareness, occasional bouts of distraction can be healthy. It's not always possible or preferable to process big feelings at the moment they arise.

The good news is that we can always regain access to our emotions. The first step is noticing when and how we repress. I spoke with some self-identified repressors to hear how they recognize when repressive tendencies are creeping in. Here's what they told me.

"The first thing I notice when I realize I am repressing my emotions is an emptiness and unresponsiveness to experiences. A void of any emotion, if you will. It feels like I am a plastic doll with a hollow center. Oftentimes, I know that I should be feeling something, anything, but the emotions never come. There is unmistakable blankness to life."

"When I notice I'm repressing something, it feels like I am trapped, like there is something propelling me to move forward but it's accompanied by a deep fear that blocks any forward motion."

"I think of my repression as a bucket. When I'm going about my day, each feeling that gets repressed fills up my bucket with just a little bit more water. The more feelings that go unprocessed and unexpressed eventually cause the bucket to fill to the brim. Once it overflows, I experience different physical symptoms such as chest pain, stomach pain, digestive issues, and fatigue."

While repression may not be the healthiest way of dealing with strong emotions, it's nothing to be ashamed of. As with anything else we want to change, we'll have an easier time working with our repression if we approach it from a stance of self-compassion (and some help from trusted others). Learning to regulate emotions rather than repress them takes time, but it's a worthwhile endeavor which ultimately helps us better understand ourselves and each other.

A NOTE ON TECHNOLOGY

Many of us use technology and social media to zone out. While this can be fine in moderation, you may want to check in with your tech use if you're a person who has a tendency to repress things. Try taking thirty-minute breaks from your phone if you suspect you're avoiding a certain feeling. Bust out your old-fashioned journal and do some self-reflective writing instead!

DO YOU SEE YOURSELF AS SOMEONE WHO REPRESSES?

IF SO, IN WHAT WAYS? HOW DO YOU BELIEVE YOU DEVELOPED THESE PATTERNS?

IF NOT, WHAT FORMS OF REGULATION WORK BEST FOR YOU?

GROWING UP, WHAT EXAMPLES DID YOU HAVE OF HEALTHY EMOTION REGULATION? WHAT EXAMPLES DID YOU HAVE OF REPRESSIVE TENDENCIES?

HOW MIGHT YOUR LIFE BE DIFFERENT IF YOU HAD A LARGER WINDOW OF TOLERANCE? WHAT DO YOU IMAGINE WOULD CHANGE FOR YOU IF YOU WERE MORE ABLE TO FEEL YOUR FEELINGS?

CRY DIARY

I STILL REMEMBER MY FIRST DIARY. IT WAS PASTEL AND IRIDESCENT (VERY '90S), AND had a large, useless lock on it that could have easily been broken by anyone who cared to try. (The metaphors abound.) I filled it with elaborate descriptions of my emotional states, writing to the very edge of the page. I usually failed to report personal events, opting instead to list each emotion's qualities in great detail like a mad scientist who had just discovered sadness and was reporting it back to the rest of humanity.

By this point in my childhood, I'd already taken to watching myself cry. There was something fascinating about seeing the way it transformed my face, how my skin would turn red in patches and my eyes looked bright green in contrast. I felt comforted by the image of my reflection, as if on some animal level it made me feel like I wasn't crying alone. As I got older, I stopped keeping a diary, but I kept watching myself cry. Even when it made me cringe, or I could hardly bear to see my reflection, I haven't looked away.

At some point, I started to document my cries. I don't really remember why (sure I do, I record everything), but I recorded myself crying on my phone. After I'd filmed a few cries, I casually organized them into a folder that I named Cry Diary. It felt like a private self-love practice to watch them back. I started to notice new faces I'd never seen myself make. I noticed how different events elicited different styles of crying, how certain phases were accompanied by more wailing or more quiet, slow cries. Little by little, I told others about my Cry Diary experiment. If the party was good enough, I'd bust a clip out for trusted friends who would always hug me and giggle, shocked I really did this. Then they'd usually joke that they were gonna start their own.

Since then, I've been lucky enough to receive other Cry Diary entries from friends and loved ones. I feel privileged to learn how their faces change, how Erik's eyelashes clump together or Marin's nose turns red at the tip. Some people make sounds when they're crying that are entirely different from anything I've heard coming out of their mouth at other times. Without fail, my fondness for them grows when I see them cry. There's something about watching a person cry that's deeply relatable and human-izing. It reminds me of the scene in *I Heart Huckabees* where Albert sees his enemy Brad crying and suddenly realizes that they are the same. A Cry Diary is a practice for learning to love ourselves more and, by extension, to see ourselves in each other. Here's how to start one of your own.

WHEN

For most of us, crying is kind of random. We can't really predict when it will occur. So step one is to decide ahead of time which device you'll use to record your next cry, then simply be prepared for that moment to strike.

WHAT

Any cell phone or laptop will work. Repeat whenever you cry. If you'd like, you can take notes about each session to track:

The date and time

The length of cry

The event that triggered the crying

How you felt before, during, and after

Any noteworthy thought processes that accompanied the cry

HOW

Let's start by establishing that crying is cool. When you think about what crying really entails, expressing your deepest feelings freely, it's pretty punk rock. But in order to be healing, it has to feel uncool. That's part of the point. When we're truly getting into it, we stop thinking about what our hair looks like or whether our biceps are ripped. This lack of inhibition is a beautiful thing in itself. It might take longer to get to this state when we're being recorded, but that's okay. If you need to, make the lighting flattering. Create a backdrop, go wild. Remember, these videos are for you. You get to decide who to share them with, and you never have to share them with anyone if you don't want to.

Once you have a few, it's time to review. This is a big moment! Your crying debut. Put on your cozy PJs. Make some popcorn and pour a glass of wine. You can play your videos on a big screen or just on your phone. Pause as needed to reflect and breathe. Let yourself feel whatever you're feeling. Do your best not to judge what comes up. Remember that watching yourself under any circumstance can be weird and uncomfortable. Even award-winning actors have a hard time watching themselves. No one ever has to see this video but you. In watching it, you can see yourself in a new light.

WHAT FEELINGS COME UP WHEN WATCHING YOURSELF CRY?

WHAT THOUGHTS ARISE?

DO YOU NOTICE ANY PATTERNS? (TIME OF CRYING, EVENTS THAT TRIGGER CRIES, FEELINGS DURING CRYING, THOUGHTS WATCHING YOURSELF CRY, ETC.)

WHO, IF ANYONE, COMES TO MIND WHEN WATCHING THESE?

IF YOU COULD SAY ANYTHING TO YOURSELF IN THE VIDEO, WHAT WOULD IT BE?

While watching yourself cry, be nice to yourself. I repeat: BE NICE TO YOUR-SELF. Look at yourself like you'd look at a person you love. Try to imagine that maybe you *are* a person you love. A person who is very deserving of your love and your curious attention.

If you feel so inclined, you can absolutely share your Cry Diary with others and ask them to do the same. If you do decide to do this, let them know ahead of time and ask for consent. Tell them what kind of feedback you're looking for, as it can be a bit awkward for some to respond to a text message that's just a video of their friend crying.

Some types of feedback you could ask for include:

Affirmations: "<3 I love you!"

Compliments: "You make such cute sounds when you're crying."

Reciprocity: "I was crying earlier today! Glad to know I'm not alone."

MAKING THE MOST OF YOUR CRYING SESSIONS

Make Crying the Goal. Imagine that crying is a game you're trying to win. The more you cry, the louder you get, the more points you're earning.

Stop Wiping Tears Away. Why do we do this? Serious question. They're not harmful, and if they're on your face they're already fucking up your makeup.

Buy Cool Handkerchiefs. It's environmentally friendly, and they have a sort of dignity to them. Plus you can pass them down through generations of sadness.

CRY PORN

Some of you may find that crying doesn't come easily. You may not cry for long periods, or find yourself unable to cry even when you want to. If so, don't feel bad! Studies have shown that the loss of the capacity to cry (or *tearlessness*) occurs in roughly 7 percent of people. There are many potential causes, not all of which are repression. SSRIs and other anxiety medications have been known to make it harder to cry. Testosterone can decrease the frequency of tears, as does gender socialization in cultures where crying is discouraged in men. Regardless of the reason, you don't need to cry to be valid. Your emotions still count. But if you do want to cry physical tears, I recommend starting a small library of cry porn. Just like the other kind of porn, this is a collection of media that helps get you in the mood.

Make a Cry Playlist. This can include music, movies, and books that have helped you cry in the past. Sometimes it's easier to cry about our own feelings through the lens of another person's story, which is part of the appeal of sad movies. Many find novels or fiction useful in this way, but music is really the one to beat here. Cry playlists all the way.

Notice Other Sensations. What other physical changes occur when you feel sad? Maybe it's not tears, but it could be the feeling of a lump in your throat. It could be your skin feeling hot. Or, as one person reported to me, an eye twitch. Notice these sensations and begin to track them. They may be the key to helping you sense when you're having the impulse to cry.

TYPES OF CRIERS

SILENT DRAMA

MOSTLY SNOT

OPERATIC

ANGRY

BLACK METAL

UGLY

MIXED FEELINGS

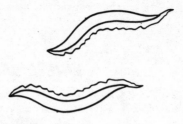

AT THE HEART OF EVERY CLASSIC DRAMA IS A CHARACTER WHO FEELS CONFLICTED. TO be or not to be? To take up the family business or venture out on my own? To marry my mom and kill my dad—or not? The reason this formula is so effective is because we all know what it's like to feel torn. We innately understand characters having mixed feelings. Yet when it comes to our own lives, we're often surprised to notice we're feeling more than one thing. We ask each other "But how do you REALLY feel?" like there's always one true feeling buried beneath the rest. One feeling may be stronger, but it doesn't mean the rest aren't real. Feeling conflicted or confused is a valid state of being. Most experiences evoke a variety of reactions in us, and an authentic response to a major event is often one of mixed emotion. As we grow older and (hopefully) wiser, our emotions become more complex. If you really think about it, almost no experience is entirely positive or negative. While researchers are still studying the physiological connection between different emotions, studies have shown that bittersweet feelings are not only common, they're beneficial.

Studies have found that mixed emotions are an indication of maturity. Researchers have also discovered that the line between pleasure and pain is quite thin, and that regular dips into bittersweet moods promote feelings of happiness, a sense of meaning in life, and even an overall increase in physical health factors. Not only that, experiencing

WHEEL OF EMOTIONS

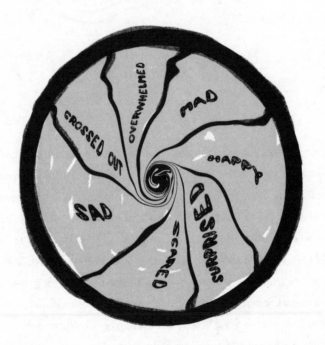

mixed feelings makes you more creative, as demonstrated by a 2018 study where researchers discovered that artists who have mixed feelings about their relationships perform better creatively. (If you're an artist, you already knew that.)

We can always increase our appreciation for these bittersweet states, but I would also point out that every one of us already enjoys some unpleasant sensations. I polled some folks about the mixed feelings they love, and here's what they said:

MIXED FEELINGS WE LOVE

- The burn of a workout
- Listening to sad music
- A good cry
- An intense massage
- Watching scary movies
- Missing someone
- The challenge of learning something new
- The bittersweet feeling of realizing everyone you love will die
- Remembering that you will die
- Caring about someone so much it hurts
- Realizing we were wrong about something and the feeling of humility that opens us up to more possibilities than we'd imagined
- Childbirth
- Looking at stars and realizing how small we are
- Overcoming a fear
- The fine line between loneliness and solitude
- Eating spicy food

WHICH OF THESE DO YOU RELATE TO? WHAT WOULD YOU ADD TO THIS LIST?

PICK ONE OF THE BITTERSWEET SENSATIONS LISTED ABOVE. WHAT ABOUT IT DO YOU ENJOY? DO YOU ASSOCIATE IT WITH ANY OTHER FEELINGS, EXPERIENCES, OR TIMES IN YOUR LIFE?

WRONG ALARM

LAST YEAR, MY FRIEND ERIK WAS ABOUT TO SPEND A WEEKEND AWAY WITH A NEW romantic partner. The two of them had never traveled together, so he was excited and nervous about the trip. Shortly after his lover arrived, Erik noticed a knot in his stomach. Being a sensitive person, he started to wonder if his intuition was telling him something was off between them, or that this weekend was a bad idea. He started to panic. He remembered all the doubts he'd had at the beginning of their relationship. "You okay?" his partner asked, able to sense that something was wrong. By this point, my friend was sweating, breathing weird, and acting even weirder. Three hours later, he was on the floor of their Airbnb bathroom with food poisoning, which is how he spent most of the weekend.

Intuition is funny like that. Sometimes our gut feelings are telling us something is wrong, and sometimes we just have gas. "Trust your gut" isn't bad advice, it's just not always possible. When people say this, what they usually mean is: Look inside yourself for the answer rather than conforming to pressure from others. I agree wholeheartedly with this sentiment, but for those of us with anxiety, trusting our gut may be easier said than done.

The reason intuition can be hard to pin down is because it isn't just one thing. Intuition is actually shorthand for an array of internal processes that are constantly taking in tons of information and trying to make sense of it. If one aspect of our intuition is out of whack, we may get faulty cues from our mind, body, or heart. We may get clear cues but not know what they're telling us to do. Our bodies have multiple internal alarm systems. They keep us alive by alerting us when we're in danger. In the case of my friend, his stomach's food poisoning alarm went off. But since he's had a number of challenging relationships in the past, he was quick to confuse his food poisoning alarm for his relationship issue alarm. There's so much going on inside of us at any given time that it's easy to do this, mistaking one alarm for another.

For those of us with a history of significant trauma, our alarms can become hyperactive. They start to interpret anything even remotely related to past hardship as a threat. Our brains and bodies get stuck in the past, either repeating memories or imagining new scenarios, trying to prepare us for any possible danger. Anyone with anxiety or PTSD knows this feeling. It can feel like there's an overactive smoke alarm inside you at all times. In the mental health world, we call it *hypervigilance*. Hypervigilance is like psychological allergies. Your nervous system is trying to keep you from experiencing trauma again, but it takes the whole effort too far. This can make it even more difficult to discern what's intuition and what's anxiety.

Part of recovering from trauma is learning to tell when our body is setting off the wrong alarm. Healing means getting better at recognizing when a feeling is tied to the present moment and when it's tied to the past. It also requires us to fine-tune our ability to sense when a feeling simply needs to be felt and when it requires action. This is a complex and personal process. Each of us must make these decisions for ourselves on a moment-to-moment basis. But the tips below can provide a starting point for checking in with ourselves when we're not sure what's being triggered in us.

Tune In to Bodily Sensations. When trying to understand a feeling, check in with your body. What physical sensations accompany it? Where do you feel it? Feelings that are trauma-based have a certain quality. They tend to flood our bodies with strong sensations right away. When a past trauma is triggered, you may suddenly feel like you're sick to your stomach, you can't breathe, or your skin is hot. If a set of bodily sensations feels familiar and immediately intense, that could be a sign that the feeling is tied to the past.

Look for Proof. Ask yourself what evidence you have that this situation is threatening. What information do you have about the events taking place that lead you to believe you're unsafe? Journaling about your feelings or speaking through them to a trusted friend can help you make sense of what exactly you're feeling threatened by.

It can also be helpful to ask others for their thoughts. Has anyone you know been through that situation? If so, what was their experience? Do they believe it to be safe for you? Consider scientific sources. Have any studies been done on the issue related to your anxiety? If so, what does that information reveal?

Consider Consistency. If a trigger is related to a specific situation or person, it won't happen just once. The feeling will be recurrent. Our bodies want to make these things loud and clear, so we will likely continue to feel the same feeling until we get the message. If you get nervous every time you're around a certain person but not around others, take note of that.

Once you establish that a certain feeling is related to the present, you may still need time to figure out what to do about it. Just because you realize that someone makes you sad or uncomfortable doesn't mean you'll instantly have clarity around how to respond. Slowing down before making decisions is part of the healing process. You don't have to know what to do right away. Just because you aren't hit with immediate clarity and crystal-clear confidence doesn't mean a situation isn't healthy or right for you. That almost never happens.

When reflection reveals that your feelings or assumptions are tied to past trauma, give yourself a high five. That's powerful self-awareness. Even when this is the case, your feelings are valid. Don't beat yourself up for feeling triggered. Now you can begin to determine what your feelings about the present situation are.

When others around you feel triggered, you may suspect that they are having a reaction based on past experience. You may want to ask if they think their history is affecting their reaction. It can be tricky to express this concern without sounding invalidating, but it's totally possible. In these moments, how you express yourself is especially important. Start by letting them know that you understand how real their feelings are for them. Remind them that you want to help. Use a soothing tone of voice. Empathize. Give them a moment to consider what you're asking.

We all need help getting perspective sometimes. We all occasionally need to be told that things aren't as bad as they seem or our wires are getting crossed. What isn't helpful is telling someone to calm down in a way that implies it should be easy for them. That's like telling someone having an allergic reaction to peanuts that they just need to breathe. Once a person knows and believes that you care and respect what's happening to them, it will be much easier for them to hear you question their intuition.

WHAT'S YOUR RELATIONSHIP TO INTUITION? DO YOU TEND TO TRUST YOUR GUT? DO YOU FIND IT EASY TO HEAR WHAT YOUR INTUITION IS TELLING YOU?

ARE THERE CERTAIN ENVIRONMENTS OR EXPERIENCES THAT MAKE IT MORE OR LESS DIFFICULT FOR YOU TO TRUST YOUR GUT? DO YOU FIND IT EASIER TO TRUST YOUR INTUITION AT WORK, IN ROMANCE, IN YOUR CREATIVE PURSUITS, ETC.?

WHAT PHYSICAL SENSATIONS DO YOU ASSOCIATE WITH INTUITION, IF ANY?

ARE THERE ANY HABITS OR BEHAVIORS THAT YOU NOTICE INCREASE YOUR ACCESS TO INTUITION?

WHAT OR WHO DO YOU TURN TO WHEN YOU DON'T FEEL LIKE YOU CAN TRUST YOUR GUT?

REFINE YOUR PAIN PALATE

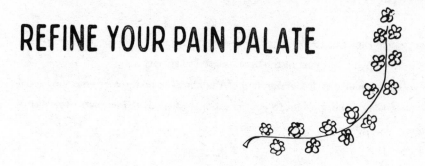

MY COUSIN LAUREN IS A SOMMELIER. SHE CAN TAKE A SIP OF WINE AND CORRECTLY identify the top and bottom notes, where the grapes were grown, even what year they were harvested. I can probably tell you whether it's red or white. That said, I can pick apart the subtle distinctions between almost any emotions. I can tell you whether what you're feeling is shame, embarrassment, or a combination. I may even be able to guess what sort of event spawned the feeling. This is because I'm a vibe connoisseur. Becoming an expert in anything means increasing your understanding of the subtleties that make it what it is.

Exploring the textures of emotion allows us to savor the subtle flavors of each. This heightened awareness makes the experience of feeling things much less confusing, and also more interesting. At first glance, it may seem like we're just feeling "good" or "bad," but when we dig in deeper, there's always more texture to our experience. Like wine, every feeling has notes, and holds a unique imprint of the time and place in which it developed.

Getting better at naming our feelings helps us understand them more deeply. Putting words to an emotion has also been shown to reduce that emotion's intensity almost instantly. Psychiatrist and author Dan Siegel refers to this method as the "name it to tame it" approach. By putting a feeling into words, we gain a sense of distance from the emotion, which allows us to examine the feeling more clearly. This process decreases activity in the amygdala, a part of the brain related to anxiety.

As you grow your own understanding of the complex textures of emotion, you'll add various feeling flavor profiles to your emotional vocabulary. Here are a few of my favorites.

ANGST

Noun, definition: a feeling of deep anxiety or dread, typically an unfocused one about the human condition or the state of the world in general.

Angst is hot. She's feisty. In the realm of shit feelings, she's the firecracker. Unlike her siblings Apathy and Malaise, Angst is in the game. She's here, she's probably queer, and she's definitely making it weird. Angst is smart and sassy. She is the energy of calling your mom out at dinner for her internalized misogyny and reminding everyone that the original Thanksgiving was a genocide. She gives a shit and will make sure that we know it (although she'll also proclaim that she doesn't care in the same breath).

Feeling profile: tangy; gritty mouthfeel; lasting aftertaste; like if you boiled longing and irritation into a soup and then added too much hot sauce

Pairs well with: impulsively shaving your head; blog posts you'll regret later; books on systemic injustice with every line highlighted

ENNUI

Noun, definition: a feeling of listlessness and dissatisfaction arising from a lack of occupation or excitement.

Ennui is dramatic. He slept until 2:00 p.m., read the entire *New York Times*, then went back to bed. He didn't apply for any jobs yesterday, but did do an unofficial lit review of all research on the extinct Carolina parakeet. He's not quite Depression, though they hang out sometimes. He's bored, but only because none of the things he could do sound fun. Ennui wants to do something big with his life, he just isn't sure what yet. He's gonna go listen to The Cure and think about it.

Feeling profile: bland; dissonant; like a mostly deflated balloon that can stay neither in the air nor on the ground

Pairs well with: half-heartedly reading books on existentialism; smoking cigarettes outside a coffee shop in the suburbs while pretending to be from France; funemployment

HUMILIATION

Noun, definition: to reduce (someone) to a lower position in one's own eyes or others' eyes, to make (someone) ashamed or embarrassed.

Humiliation is clumsy. Heavy. It feels like it could squash you, but it would definitely be an accident. Humiliation is powerful, but it doesn't know it. It's convinced that it will never belong anywhere, and it never did. Humiliation thinks of itself as a big, dumb monster, but what it doesn't know is that it's actually a powerful guardian from another land who was displaced at birth. If humiliation could only find the other freaky weirdos like itself, it could embrace its true strength. But alas, it may be destined for awkwardness.

Feeling profile: like putting your clothes on while they're wet and then sitting in a room that's either very hot or very cold until they dry

Pairs well with: the fetal position; eating ice cream in bed; picking up the phone and throwing it back down over and over

---

CREATE YOUR OWN! HOW WOULD YOU DESCRIBE LONELINESS, DREAD, PANIC, OR SOME OTHER EMOTION?

WHAT KIND OF PERSONALITY DO YOU IMAGINE IT HAVING?

WHAT DOES IT FEEL LIKE IN YOUR BODY?

WHAT ACTIVITIES PAIR WELL WITH IT?

MESSY MINDFULNESS

I LOVE TO MEDITATE. WAIT, LET ME REPHRASE THAT: I LOVE HOW MEDITATION MAKES me feel. A meditation practice has been shown to calm the nervous system, sharpen insight, and increase overall well-being. There was a time in my life when I was meditating a lot, like in the formal, sit-on-a-cushion-in-a-quiet-room kind of way. As I got older and my life became more chaotic, however, I started shortening my sits. Then skipping days. Like many people, my schedule is often so stuffed that even pausing to eat can feel like a luxury. I travel often and don't always have access to a quiet place. I realized that if I was struggling to commit to a formal daily practice myself, others probably were as well.

As a therapist, it's all well and good for me to encourage my clients to meditate and do yoga every day since I know there are real mental health benefits to these endeavors. At the same time, I've come to understand that much of modern meditation training (and healing work in general) is built on assumptions that aren't true for everyone. Like that people have time to meditate regularly, or that they have a place in which to do it. Even the assumption that people have the mental capacity to sit without falling asleep can feel presumptuous in this era, but I still think it's worth striving for. While ideal conditions may not be available to all of us, that doesn't mean that we can't experience the benefits of mindfulness. It may just get a bit messy.

One thing to remember is that meditation and mindfulness are not the same. Meditation is a practice, while mindfulness is a state of being. We hope that seated meditation will make us more mindful, but it's not the only way to develop this skill. When we're mindful, we're able to pay attention to what's happening both inside of us and around us. As valuable as mindfulness is, it's not a panacea. It's important that we understand what mindfulness is and it is not before embarking on an attempt to pursue it.

MINDFULNESS IS NOT

having no thoughts

feeling perpetually peaceful

never getting distracted

MINDFULNESS IS

focusing on one thing at a time

not judging thoughts and feelings

coming back to the moment

While it won't solve all your problems, mindfulness is a skill worth developing. People often tell me they can't meditate or do other mindfulness-enhancing practices because their minds are too busy. When they say this, what I actually hear is that they could benefit from meditation. Brains are busy by nature. As a mental health professional and meditation practitioner, I can confirm that it's very hard to get your brain to shut up. Brains don't want to do that. They want to make thoughts (an estimated thirty thousand to seventy thousand a day, although exact figures are contested). Meditation won't make your brain stop, but it will help you put some space between your thoughts.

As we become more mindful, we become more present in our lives. We gain the ability to recognize what is actually happening in the current moment. As discussed, it can be tough to know whether an emotion is rooted in the past or the present, or is an attempt at forecasting the future. Being present helps us get clearer about this, which then helps us choose our behavior more consciously. As we become more present, we will likely notice how often we are distracted or lost in random rabbit holes. Often, we are not actually paying attention to the situation we're in, and may be oblivious to the tangible sights, sounds, and smells of the reality our bodies are occupying. Mindfulness helps us orient ourselves to the here and now.

The world is rarely serene. Most of us aren't living in monasteries, and, if we're lucky enough to have the time and space to meditate, we may still be hearing our roommates fight or smelling our neighbor's weed smoke. Such is life. This anytime-anywhere meditation practice is designed to help you become more mindful, even if your circumstances aren't ideal.

♥ Start by lowering your gaze. You don't need to close your eyes, but let them relax. Allow them to stop focusing for now, and instead take in information passively. Lower your shoulders and unclench your jaw. Get more comfortable in your seat.

♥ Take a moment to notice where you are. Go through a mental checklist, answering each of these questions either aloud or in your mind:

Who am I?

Where am I?

What day is it?

What am I doing right now?

(OBVIOUSLY, PUT YOUR PHONE AWAY WHILE MEDITATING OR PRACTICING MINDFULNESS.)

I know it might sound ridiculous, but humor me.

Here's mine: I'm Chelsea. I'm in a café in Montreal. It's Monday at 10:28 a.m. I'm writing a book.

Now, you try.

♥ Next, take three deep breaths and try to lengthen your exhale each time.

♥ Once you're done with that, shift your attention to the lowest parts of your body, whichever part is touching the ground. Keep breathing, obviously. Let yourself move your relaxed, curious attention to the sensations of that part of your body. If you're walking, feel your feet on the sidewalk. If you're sitting, feel your body being supported by the chair or grass or concrete or whatever is beneath you. Don't overthink the sensations. Just notice them. Do this for as long as you want to.

♥ Rinse and repeat.

AGONY ALTAR

THE FIRST TIME I BUILT AN AGONY ALTAR, I DIDN'T REALIZE THAT'S WHAT I WAS doing. I was between jobs, living alone in my hometown. I'd had to quit school because I couldn't afford tuition and was struggling to make rent. After she'd been sober for a time, I'd invited my mom to move in with me (the only time we'd lived together since infancy) but soon after, she relapsed and left abruptly. As one might suspect, this brought up a lot of feelings. One night, I was crying in my bedroom. I'd gotten used to doing that in private so as to avoid disturbing her, but it suddenly dawned on me that I was alone. I could cry anywhere!

I crawled to the living room and curled up next to the window. It was spring and the air was sweet. I let the curtains blow in the breeze. Basically, I just sat there and cried. Soon, I found myself gathering mementos and assembling them there like a sad squirrel. I propped the few photos I had of us together next to journal entries, poems I'd scribbled on receipts, even old stuffed animals. For weeks, I perched in front of it and watched the sunset through my wet eyelashes.

Only later did I realize I'd built an altar. Having not attended much church in my life, I hadn't been exposed to many conventional altars. As I started getting more involved in paganism and healing circles, I noticed there was almost always an altar at events. I was and still am perpetually drawn to them. I find myself fascinated by the things people choose to display, and how placing something on an altar seems to transform it into a treasure. Altars can make any event feel sacred, even if that event is sitting on the ground and feeling bad for yourself. There's something surprisingly dignifying about kneeling before an altar. Through years of engagement with them, I've come to understand that altars help us process big emotions by making the ineffable real and therefore less intimidating.

The more I studied ritual, the more I learned that altars are a universal, ancient tool for directing energy. For most of human history, people from cultures all over the world have built them. Typically involved in spiritual ceremony, altars can serve as metaphorical portals for processing strong emotions and transmuting painful energy. Depending on your belief, altars can help you commemorate milestones, communicate with your guides, and process grief. Here's a guide to building one of your own.

WHERE

Ideally, your agony altar will be somewhere in your home that's private and can be dedicated to this purpose specifically. You shouldn't need more than a corner. An unused closet can also be great. If you don't have a space at home, consider a portable altar. For this, you'll fill a bag with your objects and bring it to an area where you feel a sense of both spaciousness and safety. Maybe it's a local park or favorite hiking spot. If anyone asks what you're carrying, tell them it's a bag filled with agony. That should end any unwanted conversation.

What's most important is that the space where you build your altar is somewhere that offers the freedom to get creative and room to sit and feel. And, you know, ugly cry in peace. Once you've chosen your spot, you can start selecting your items.

WHAT

You can decorate your altar with anything, but try to choose artifacts that hold emotional significance for you. Start thinking about whether you want your altar to be centered around an event, theme, or feeling. Allow your mind to wander on the subject of despair.

What comes up for you? Is it memories of a difficult experience, like a heartbreak or loss? Is it feelings centered around a theme or issue you've struggled with, such as body image or addiction? Is it a subject you're passionate about, like animal cruelty or climate change? Trust it.

Once you've selected the focus, think about what items symbolize that theme. If your altar is centered around mourning an event in your childhood, you might want to decorate it with photos of yourself from that age, toys, or pictures of the people you looked up to then. If your altar is based on a feeling, ask yourself some questions about it:

What are the qualities of this feeling?

Is it fluid like water or rigid like stone?

Does it have a color?

Does it have a shape?

Is it heavy or light?

What is its size, texture?

Are there any images, objects, sounds associated with this pain?

There are no wrong answers. Anything that comes to mind can help inspire which items you select. If none of these questions work for you, simply choose items based on what feels most interesting and meaningful.

Some items to consider including:

- *Photos of loved ones who have left your life or passed away*
- *Self-portraits and drawings*
- *Leaves, plants, or flowers (fresh or dried)*
- *Herbs and tinctures*
- *Quotes and passages from mentors, guides, or anyone who inspires you*
- *Candles, potpourri, or incense*
- *Poems and old journal entries*
- *Fabric, yarn, or items of clothing you wore during significant events*

- *Bones, dead butterflies, anything a creepy child would collect*
- *Stones, rocks, or crystals*
- *Images from magazines*
- *Mementos or relics from your early years*
- *Jewelry or items of family significance*
- *Snacks*

Before assembling, you may also want to get your hands on some basic decorating tools like markers, paint, glitter, and a glue gun. You'll likely need something structural to set your altar on. The easiest choice is an end table with fabric draped over it, but feel free to get creative.

HOW

You're building an altar of despair. You're bravely facing your inner demons. You're starting to worry you won't get your deposit back. Before beginning construction, consider whether you need to put down a tarp. Depending on how far you're going, put on some crappy clothes while you put it together.

If possible, set aside a few hours for construction. Gather everything you anticipate needing ahead of time. This is self-care, so make the process therapeutic. Create a playlist of songs that help evoke the right mood. Make a tasty little beverage. Enjoy!

Once you've built your altar, you get to decide how you'll use it. There are many practices to choose from. Some classics include:

- *Journaling*
- *Coloring*

- *Meditating*
- *Singing*
- *Reading tarot cards*
- *Gazing into the abyss (I hear it gazes back)*

You can choose to sit in front of your altar every day, once a week, or as needed. Whatever you choose to do, don't stress about it. This is not about perfection or strict adherence to a rule, it's about honoring a feeling that so rarely gets its time. Have fun! But not too much fun, this is about pain.

LIVE LAUGH LEAVE ME ALONE

UNLEARNING THE IMPULSE TO ISOLATE

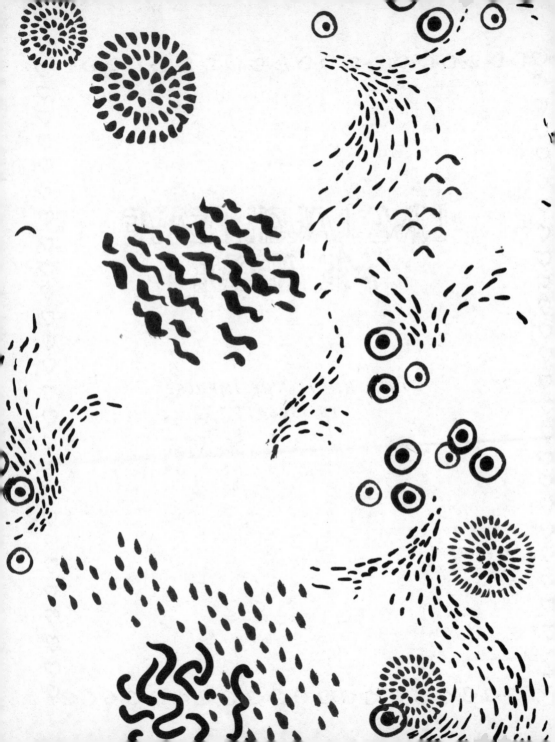

IN DEFENSE OF DEBBIE DOWNER

> If you are silent about your pain, they'll kill
> you and say you enjoyed it.
>
> —Zora Neale Hurston

ONE WAY TO REALLY GET ON MY NERVES IS TO MOCK SOMEONE WHO'S "CRYING FOR HELP." That's literally the point of crying. If our ancestors didn't cry, we might not be alive today. So yes, cry for help. And be grateful when others do because it keeps our whole species alive.

Crying alone is great, but crying with others is better. Not just crying, but venting, making shameful confessions, and saying the things we're scared to say. Generally speaking, this style of communication is discouraged. Don't be a downer, we're told. Keep it light, they say. But research has shown that those who engage in small talk are less satisfied with life than those who discuss deep issues. Talking about our problems with others reduces physical and emotional distress almost instantly, while hiding what we feel triggers a stress response in both the person suppressing their emotions as well as the person they're keeping them from. Crying in the presence of a supportive person also makes us feel better than crying alone and opens up the possibility for deeper connection to form.

Beyond the interpersonal, causing a fuss helps move society forward. Without dissenters, we would rarely make progress. We need those brave people who are unsatisfied, who refuse to accept the status quo and are willing to say this is not good enough. We deserve better. No matter who you are or where you live, your life is better because of people like this who came before you.

We also need Debbie Downers to help us mourn. When it comes to grieving, public crying was once honored as a social service. Even today, there are places in the world where professional mourning, aka moirology, is still a valid profession. These people are my heroes. Is there anything more metal than getting paid to weep? As one of the world's oldest jobs, moirologists, aka expert criers, have existed across cultures throughout human history. In ancient Egypt, professional mourners were understood to be representatives of the goddesses Isis and Nephthys. They stood at either end of a coffin during funeral services and wailed or knelt over the body. In ancient Rome, paid grievers made up a large percentage of the funeral procession. The more people openly mourning a person, the higher their social status was understood to be. Today, in England, you can still hire a moirologist from a business called Rent-A-Mourner. In China, a well-known professional griever named Hu Xinglian travels often to do this work, and has become known for her theatrical displays.

Many of us living today might find these customs strange. But we also likely know the relief of seeing someone cry when we're trying to hold it in. By openly crying first, these people give the rest of us permission to release what's stuck inside. By going over the top in their expressions of despair, they lower the stakes for others so we can lose ourselves without standing out. There's something profoundly life affirming about witnessing another person's full display of despair, validating just how deep the well of human hurt can go.

Even when mourning hasn't been compensated financially, it has often been revered. Through various cultures, crying has been seen as spiritually and morally significant in a variety of ways. Shia Muslims think of crying as a duty toward past spiritual teachers who have experienced religious persecution as it shows gratitude and reverence. In Orthodox Christianity and Catholicism, crying is considered a show of sincere repentance for sins. While we've come to regard expressing feelings of sadness as weak, it's often the opposite. The person who is strong enough to feel it shows others how to move through that energy.

I have a client named Sonya whose brother is in the process of dying. Her family has endured multiple tragedies already, so when they got the news about Ted, everyone felt totally defeated and unsure if they could handle another loss. Throughout the process, Sonya has been the one most able to express her sadness. She feels insecure about this. In one of our recent sessions, she was discussing an upcoming trip to visit her brother and family. No one knows how much time he has, and she was worried she wouldn't be able to "keep it together" if she went.

"I'll just be crying the whole time, I know it." She was crying as she said this. "I don't want to make it all about me. I'm not the one dying, after all. If everyone else can hold their feelings in, shouldn't I do that, too?" I let silence hold her question for a moment, then asked:

"If you were dying and nobody around you was crying, how would you feel?" She laughed through tears and said, "Point made."

Most of us can relate to Sonya's thinking here. We don't cry publicly because we don't want to "make it about us," but often, it's already about us. When loss touches a person or community we're tied to, an authentic expression of sadness isn't selfish, it's honoring. Trying to avoid being distressed only acts to remove us from the situation. When we equate apathy with strength, we set a trap for ourselves. Disengagement may be rewarded with respect, but relationships require responsiveness. We can't have meaningful connections without opening ourselves up to being impacted by others, and being prepared to impact them.

Another common misunderstanding is that expressing sadness in front of others means that we're making a request or asking them to resolve it for us. This is not the case. When we cry, we're simply allowing our bodies to show what's happening inside of us. It's no more a request than laughing or dancing in front of someone is a request. Asking for help is important, too, but expressing sadness and asking for support are different things.

When we can let ourselves be the Debbie Downer, the one who's brave enough to show how we're feeling, we may actually be doing a public service. By shamelessly expressing our most vulnerable feelings, we may be helping others embrace their hard feelings as well. So let it out. Let others see that you're affected by life. And remember that, by doing so, you may be changing the world.

WHAT ARE YOUR BELIEFS ABOUT EXPRESSING NEGATIVE EMOTIONS IN FRONT OF OTHERS?

WHAT DEBBIE DOWNERS ARE YOU GRATEFUL FOR?

CAN YOU THINK OF A PERSONAL, PROFESSIONAL, OR PUBLIC EXAMPLE OF A TIME WHEN SOMEONE WAS VOCAL ABOUT A DIFFICULT EXPERIENCE AND THEIR OPENNESS HELPED YOU FEEL LESS ALONE OR EMPOWERED TO SPEAK UP FOR YOURSELF?

PUBLIC CRYING BINGO

AT YOUR EX'S WEDDING	IN A BANK LOBBY	AT A HAIR SALON	ON A FIRST DATE	AT A CONCERT
AT DINNER WITH YOUR FAMILY	AT DINNER WITH SOMEONE ELSE'S FAMILY	WHILE LIFTING WEIGHTS AT THE GYM	IN AN UBER	ON STAGE
AT YOUR OWN BIRTHDAY PARTY	AT THE DENTIST	THERAPY WAITING ROOM	HIDING IN A CLOSET (DRUNK)	HIDING IN A CLOSET (SOBER)
ON A CROWDED SUBWAY	AT THE DMV	AIRPORT	ON AN IKEA DISPLAY COUCH	IN SOMEONE ELSE'S YARD
ART MUSEUM	POLLING BOOTH	PETTING A STRANGER'S DOG / CAT	PARKED AT AN INTERSECTION	BATHROOM STALL AT WORK

ATTENTION IS NUTRITIOUS

ATTENTION IS A BASIC NEED. AS SOCIAL CREATURES, WE NEED ATTENTION FROM others the same way we need shelter. We can survive without it for a while, but we won't be well. We tend to think of attention as something we need only when we're young, but that's not true. We need attention at every age. Not all attention is created equal, however. Like food, everyone's attention offers different nutrients.

In addition to offering different kinds of attention, we all tend to want different types, too. If you're not sure what kind of attention someone in your life is desiring, notice what they offer. We generally give the kind of attention we want, so if someone gives a lot of positive reinforcement, they likely want that, too. If someone provides a lot of deep, reflective comments, they may want those back from you. You can also always ask.

THE LOVING PARENT
- - - - - - - - - - - - - -

Nutrition Facts

Serving size   15 minutes

Amount per serving
Emotional Calories   **430**

% Daily Value*

Believing in your
potential even when you
repeatedly waste it   **84%**

Making you feel like you're
doing them a favor when you
tell them about your day **27%**

Knowing you're hungry
before you do   **52%**

Free snacks   **72%**

* The % Daily Value (DV) tells you how much a nutrient
contributes to a daily diet.

THE BEST FRIEND
- - - - - - - - - - - - - -

Nutrition Facts

Serving size   15 minutes

Amount per serving
Emotional Calories   **280**

% Daily Value*

Loving you at your most
unhinged   **87%**

Staying on the phone with
you for three hours while
you run errands   **44%**

Respectfully calling
you on your bullshit   **37%**

Hating your enemies   **17%**

Stopping you from
making horrible choices **14%**

* The % Daily Value (DV) tells you how much a nutrient
contributes to a daily diet.

THE COMMITTED PARTNER
- - - - - - - - - - - - - - - - - -

Nutrition Facts

Serving size   15 minutes

Amount per serving
Emotional Calories   **310**

% Daily Value*

Permission to cry   **20%**
Knowing how to calm you down **42%**

Listening without
offering unsolicited advice **65%**

Thinking you look beautiful
when you absolutely do not **71%**

Foot massages   **87%**

Ability and willingness
to discuss their feelings
and needs   **200%**

* The % Daily Value (DV) tells you how much a nutrient
contributes to a daily diet.

THE GOOD ROOMMATE
- - - - - - - - - - - - - - - -

Nutrition Facts

Serving size   15 minutes

Amount per serving
Emotional Calories   **210**

% Daily Value*

Direct communication about
household issues before
they become a big deal   **67%**

Casual invitations to tag
along to events without
pressuring you to hang   **43%**

Cleaning the toilet   **27%**

Respecting your privacy
when you leave your
journal on the coffee table **19%**

* The % Daily Value (DV) tells you how much a nutrient
contributes to a daily diet.

WHAT QUALITIES DO YOU THINK YOUR ATTENTION OFFERS?

WHAT QUALITIES DO THOSE IN YOUR LIFE BRING?

WHAT KIND OF ATTENTION DO YOU CRAVE MOST?

WHAT KIND OF ATTENTION IS MOST LACKING IN YOUR LIFE?

WHAT KIND IS MOST ABUNDANT?

LISTEN BUDDY

MOST OF US THINK WE'RE GOOD LISTENERS. MOST OF US ARE NOT GOOD LISTENERS. Part of the reason people get this wrong is because we mistakenly assume that listening is simple. We think that as long as we're not talking over someone, we're listening to them. Not quite. In truth, listening involves a number of skills. Listening well is not just about our external behavior, it's about our internal posture. To be an active listener is to genuinely become curious about what others are thinking and feeling, even if we don't automatically feel interested. This can take a bit of effort, but it ultimately brings about many rewards.

Active listening is, well, active. It's not simply receiving information; it's engaging with that information. Active listeners "amplify, energize, and clarify" what speakers say. They offer feedback, but they do so cautiously, sensitively, and in a way that reflects an understanding of the speaker's goals. Active listening impacts both the listener and the listened to. The more we feel heard, the more willing we are to cooperate with someone. This is why listening is such a powerful tool for change. Listening to someone, even via an audio recording, syncs our brain waves to mimic theirs. This means that listening to others is one way to shift our own mental state and get out of our heads.

When we really listen to someone else, we create the potential to be transformed by what they share. We can't listen well unless we're willing to be altered, either through a change in our emotional state or exposure to a worldview that challenges our own. This may be why many people are afraid to truly listen. Listening takes courage. It takes flexibility. It asks us to leave our thoughts behind for a time and consider someone else's. We can always come back to our own thoughts, of course, but we may do so with information that expands or shifts our thinking.

Active listening takes full engagement. When we're distracted, either by stimulus in our environment or our own mental meandering, we can't really hear what the other person is saying. Listening requires us to pause and give our attention to the speaker. Part of active listening is knowing when we are and are not able to listen well. If we're distracted, we can let our conversational partner know this. Then we can take the time to become more prepared to listen, and let them know when we're ready. Here are some tips for improving listening skills.

HOW TO LISTEN WELL

Stay Engaged. Active listening involves letting the speaker know we're engaged with what they're sharing. We can do this in a number of ways, verbally or nonverbally: nodding, smiling or laughing at funny comments, quietly saying "mm-hmm" or "interesting," and other subtle signs that we're following along.

Don't Try to Fix It. Most people don't want advice. Listening and giving advice aren't mutually exclusive, but it's much easier for someone to hear our suggestions if they feel we've fully listened first. Active listening requires us to understand what someone is saying before trying to help them solve a problem. Ideally, we will check in about the kind of feedback they're looking for before offering a response. We can ask: "What sort of feedback would be most useful? I'm happy to just listen, or I can help you brainstorm solutions."

Ask Questions. People feel more heard by someone who asks open-ended, nonjudgmental questions when they're speaking. These questions can demonstrate our curiosity and understanding by reflecting back what we've heard them say and inquiring about another facet of the subject.

You may be wondering: What if I'm genuinely not interested? That's okay, no one is automatically interested in everything. But active listening does sometimes involve conjuring interest by finding some part of what the speaker is sharing that we're curious about, or even something we don't quite understand, and asking a question about that.

Reflect. Another key feature of active listening is assessing for understanding. Active listeners don't take it personally when they miss something. Instead, they give the speaker the chance to fill in the gaps by reflecting back what they think they heard and asking for confirmation. This might sound like: "I'm hearing that you're feeling frustrated and you're considering leaving your job. Is that right?" This gives the speaker the chance to clarify, adjust, or validate what the listener takes away from their share.

Empathize. This might sound obvious, but active listening isn't judgmental. Perhaps above all, active listening involves empathy. People tend to feel most heard when someone is truly aligning with their perspective, at least for the time when they are speaking. This scares many people as there are lots of misconceptions about what empathy is and is not.

ON EMPATHY

Empathy is the ability to understand and feel what it would be like to be someone else. Since everyone is unique, it takes empathy to fully imagine another being's experience, let alone care about it. Psychologists Daniel Goleman and Paul Ekman have added texture to this definition, outlining three specific forms of empathy: cognitive, emotional, and compassionate. Cognitive empathy involves accurately perceiving what another person's experience is like, in terms of understanding their perspective and motivations. Emotional empathy involves feeling similar feelings ourselves, while compassionate empathy means that we actively care about the other's experience and even want to improve it. Empathy may seem complicated, but don't overthink it. Here are some simple ways to clarify what empathy is and is not.

Empathy is:

interest in someone's experience
a desire to understand why they think how they do
concern about how they feel

Empathy is not:

agreement with someone's opinion
a commitment to help them solve an issue
condoning behaviors they act on in response to their feeling

To empathize with someone is not to sign up to be with them through the long haul. It's not an endorsement of them or their work in the world. It's not even a belief that their feelings are reasonable. Empathy is just understanding. It's imagining how the world feels and seems to another being. Empathy can be restricted to the moments when we're listening. Once we're done trying to empathize, we may decide that we think the person we were empathizing with is an asshole and we don't want to talk to them ever again. But for that moment, we heard and hopefully understood them.

As empathy and listening both involve a variety of subtle skills, it's likely that we're better at some than others. If we want to expand our expertise in this arena, we can start by taking stock of what areas we excel in already and which need the most work.

WHICH ASPECTS OF LISTENING ARE YOU BEST AT? WHICH COULD USE THE MOST WORK?

WHAT FORMS OF EMPATHY COME MOST NATURALLY TO YOU? WHAT FORMS FEEL MOST DIFFICULT?

WHO IN YOUR LIFE HAS MADE YOU FEEL MOST HEARD? IN WHAT WAYS?

WHO IN YOUR LIFE DOESN'T LISTEN TO YOU WELL? WHAT DO YOU WISH THEY DID MORE OF?

A NOTE ON SHAME SPIRALS

When it comes to listening, trust me, you will fuck it up. We all will. We will accidentally interrupt, we'll say something offensive, or we'll fail to ask how others are feeling. No matter how good we get at communicating, we mess up. Just yesterday, in the midst of a very cold month of quarantining at home, I complained about having cabin fever to my disabled grandfather, who has been confined to one room in a nursing home for four years. As soon as I started venting about how I missed going for drives (which I did somewhat recently! Just not recently enough for my liking!), we both started laughing because we realized how extremely inconsiderate I was being by complaining about this to him. Rather than falling into a "shame spiral" and asking him to tell me I'm not selfish when we both knew I was just being selfish, I just apologized and moved on.

When you notice you're doing something disrespectful (or someone else graciously alerts you to it), the best thing to do is notice it, acknowledge it, and move on. This can be easier said than done. For many of us, guilt quickly becomes shame. As researcher Brené Brown points out, guilt is the belief that we did something bad, while shame makes us believe that we are bad. When the recognition that we might have done something hurtful spirals into "I'm a horrible person" . . . "Why do people even hang out with me" . . . and "omg, I'm the worst" in our minds, it becomes much more difficult to repair the damage we've just done.

Once we've slipped into a shame spiral, we will likely start to lob accusations against ourselves that are too painful to accept, then feel we need to defend against those even though the other person probably did not actually say or think those things. At this point, we're having the wrong kind of pity party. In doing this, we're actually making the moment more about us. This is called *hijacking the interaction*. And while it may have started as an innocent observation that we'd been shitty, it's often even shittier than just acknowledging what we did and letting it go.

Putting ourselves down might seem like a humbling thing to do, but it's actually a way of deflecting responsibility. Denial is closer to arrogance than accountability, because it implies that we don't think it's possible that we made a mistake. Deeper still, denial can indicate that our self-esteem is fragile, as it suggests that we can like ourselves only if we're perfect. When we become defensive, hijack the interaction, or fall into a shame spiral, we're telling others that our ego is so weak that we can't handle hearing how we made them feel. We don't have to agree with other people's assessment of what we did, but we don't actually get to disagree with how we made them feel. That's not up to us.

When it comes to listening, our insecurity doesn't help anyone. It actually makes it harder for us to focus on others because we're so focused on how we might mess up and what it will mean if we do. Let's just accept that we will, and that we'll learn from our blunders as we go. Here are some tips for getting out of a shame spiral if someone's critical feedback has you falling into one.

Slow Down. Notice what's happening in your body. Take a couple deep breaths before responding. Feel the chair beneath you if you're sitting and the ground beneath your feet.

Own It. Assuming the person you're talking with isn't a total jerk, it can be really helpful just to let them know you're feeling triggered and need a minute. Better that than denying it and slipping into self-loathing silently.

Empathize with Yourself. You may have done something hurtful, but that doesn't mean you're worthless or bad. We all mess up. If you feel so inclined, place your hand on your chest. Feel your heart beating and remember your own tenderness. Quickly attuning to your own needs makes it easier to return to another person's.

Thank Them. If you're responding to what someone else said, acknowledge that you hear them. You're not agreeing, you're just letting them know you'll think about what they shared. If you actually don't understand what they're saying and need more information, ask for clarity but PROCEED WITH CAUTION! This should be an actual question, not a defense disguised as a question.

Real Question: "Would you be willing to give me a little more information about what I said or did that felt dismissive?"

Fake Question: "Can you please give me some proof that I was being dismissive because I'm pretty sure I always listen to you even though you never stop talking."

Brevity is your friend here.

Process Later. If you're still feeling triggered, you don't have to sort it out at this moment. You can always process later by talking with another trusted friend or therapist, or by journaling.

THE SILENT TREATMENT

SILENCE IS A NATURAL OCCURRENCE IN CONVERSATION. IN A SOCIETY AS OVERSTIMULAT-ing as ours, shared silence can be a rare and beneficial break from the near-constant mental and physical chatter. For me, nothing is quite as cozy as the silence of an old friend or lover reading a book by my side. That said, there are many forms of silence, not all of which are pleasant. There's the awkward silence between acquaintances, the tense silence between ex-lovers, and the horrifying silence between my supervisor and me after I accidentally sent her a selfie while drunk. There are also silences that don't convey comfort or discomfort but rather reflect a lack of relationship, like the dead air between strangers on a train or the oddly intimate silence between you and your Uber driver on a long ride home. Regardless of the type, silence is an important part of conversation, and how we work with silence has a lot to do with how well we can co-regulate with others.

Most of us could use some help embracing silence. Intentional silences can be therapeutic, letting us toggle between attending to what another person is feeling and what we're feeling. Many of us exist in a state of mild dysregulation much of the time, which compromises our ability to stay present. We often find that we can't pay attention to our own feelings until we're alone because others are continuously talking at us. If we can pause a conversation long enough to check in with ourselves while with other people, we can become more present, making our time spent connecting much richer. In order to do this, we need to learn to be okay with silence.

TIPS FOR MANAGING SHARED SILENCE

Look Within. Check in with yourself. When you notice that silence is getting awkward, turn your attention inward. Ask yourself if there's something else making you uncomfortable in that moment. Do a quick scan of your body, taking stock of any noteworthy sensations. Close your eyes if you need to. Breathe.

Relax Your Muscles. Unclench your jaw. Deepen your breath. Lower your shoulders and remember you're not responsible for other people's experience. You don't have to speak just to fill the space.

Hum. Or make another kind of small sound on your exhale. This signals to your body and the bodies of those around you that your silence means you're calm, not hostile.

Communicate Nonverbally. Smile. Place your hand on the other person's shoulder if that's comfortable for you both. Adjust your position to feel most comfortable. Lie down on the ground. Curl up in the fetal position if you need to. Do you.

Speak Slowly. It's hard to process verbal information in a dysregulated state, so even our most brilliant affirmations may be lost on someone who's processing an intense emotion. That said, low-pressure, reassuring statements like "Thanks for being vulnerable with me" and "I'm not going anywhere" can help someone feel safe in shared silence. Practice attuning to whether others are craving silence or encouragement.

Ask to Pause. If you notice that you need a break from speaking during conversation, let the person you're talking with know this by calmly saying, "I'm just gonna take a moment to breathe." Close your eyes and take three deep, slow breaths. If they seem concerned, let them know that pausing during conversation helps you stay in a regulated state.

Invite Others to Pause. If you notice that someone you're speaking with seems hurried or distracted, gently invite them to take a break from speaking. You can do this by simply saying "Take your time" if they're speaking quickly and then slowing down your own speech, movements, and breathing.

WHAT IS YOUR RELATIONSHIP WITH SILENCE? IS IT EASY OR HARD FOR YOU TO BE SILENT WITH OTHERS?

HOW DID YOUR FAMILY RELATE TO SILENCE WHEN YOU WERE GROWING UP? WAS SHARED SILENCE COMMON? IF SO, WAS IT COMFORTABLE, AWKWARD, HOSTILE, OR SOMETHING ELSE?

ARE THERE ANY RELATIONSHIPS IN YOUR LIFE YOU THINK WOULD BENEFIT FROM MORE SHARED SILENCE? IF SO, WHICH OF THE TIPS ABOVE MIGHT YOU USE TO TRY INCORPORATING MORE SILENCE INTO THAT CONNECTION?

EVERYONE IS NEEDY

"I don't want to be a burden."

"I hope I didn't bother anybody."

"I'm just too needy."

People sometimes apologize for talking about themselves and their needs . . . in therapy sessions. As endearing as that may sound, I find it troubling. We've been raised to see being needy as so shameful that it's almost as if there's no context in which we find it appropriate (even when receiving mental health care). None of us wants to be a burden to others, and yet the reality is that we all are at some point. Living beings have needs, and most of those needs are met by engaging with something outside ourselves.

We eat food from the earth. We live in cities others built. We take life-saving medicines that other people produce. Everybody is a burden and everybody is a benefit because it takes a whole community to keep one person alive. Every one of us is a part of that community. By virtue of existing, we take up space. We have needs. And we each have just as much of a right to have them met as any other being on the planet.

Yes, it's scary to have needs. It means we have to depend on others for our survival. Life would feel a lot safer if we could just subsist entirely on our own, but we can't.

The bad news is we're gonna keep being needy. The good news is everyone is in that same boat with us. In the words of therapist Stan Tatkin, "There's no such thing as a low-maintenance person up close." When someone seems like they don't have needs, that's likely because

- *their needs are already being met*
- *they're repressing their needs*
- *they're not revealing their needy side (yet)*

People fitting into category A are usually people with an immense amount of social privilege. It's easy not to notice your needs when they're being accommodated. If you've been lucky long enough, you might not even know you have needs! But that's like thinking you don't get hungry because you've always had enough to eat. If you stopped having food, you'd get just as hungry as the rest of us.

People in group B may have had their needs neglected or ignored as children. They may therefore have developed avoidant attachment styles. If you've never heard of attachment styles, then you are hanging out in a very different corner of the internet than I am. Attachment styles are part of attachment theory, a framework developed by psychiatrist John Bowlby and psychologist Mary Ainsworth for understanding how humans' early relationships with caregivers produce certain patterns that persist throughout life. What they found was that the way a baby's needs are met (or not met) greatly affects their behavior in future relationships, as well as how they regulate emotion. The four attachment styles are:

Secure: People who have a secure attachment style (an estimated 50 percent of the general population) had caregivers who were "good enough." They were physically and emotionally present most of the time, leading the child to believe it was safe to depend on others, which in turn made them feel more confident exploring the world. As adults, people who have a secure attachment style feel more comfortable balancing both the need for closeness and the need for autonomy within relationships. They still feel anxious, rejected, smothered, and all the other things humans in relationships feel, but because of those early experiences of relational safety, they're generally able to deal with those feelings and work to find win-win solutions.

Avoidant: People with avoidant attachment styles (roughly 25 percent of the population) had caregivers who were either physically or emotionally absent a large part of the time or smothering and overly protective. Either of these extremes can create a situation where a child feels unsafe asking for their needs to be met, either because it resulted in rejection in their early life or because asking for help from the parent meant that the child's boundaries would be violated and their personal space intruded upon. When this happens, a child copes by repressing the internal signal telling them that they need something. As it is too painful to continue being shut down or smothered by a caregiver, the child simply tunes those cues out. This provides temporary respite from negative feelings, but results in less awareness of one's needs. In adulthood, this manifests as a general disregard for intimate relationships, a fear of depending on others, and a persistent need for space.

Anxious: Those who develop an anxious style (about 20 percent of people) had parents who were unpredictable. They were present and comforting some of the time, and cold or stress-inducing at other times. Perhaps these caregivers had difficulty regulating their emotions themselves. This results in a tendency for children to feel ambivalent about needing things from their caregiver. Because the behavior is chaotic and difficult to make sense of, the child places an undue amount of attention on the adult's behavior, trying to predict what will or won't make them available in their time of need. In adult relationships, this results in an extreme focus on their relational partner's patterns, feelings of jealousy and anxiety that they will leave, and difficulty regulating one's own emotions.

Disorganized: People who form a disorganized style (about 5 percent) grew up in environments that are often highly alarming or frightening. When a caregiver presents a child with contradictory messages (holding them close, while also being physically or emotionally cruel), that confuses the child and overwhelms their system. The impulse to seek closeness and safety with another human is innate and hardwired. Because of this, the disorganized child feels the desire to be close to the adult but also fears them. As an adult, this can result in a feeling of being trapped when connected with others but also longing for that feeling of safety one did not experience in their early years.

All attachment styles are adaptations. They are coping skills developed in response to our environment. As adults, we almost all have one dominant style, but we experience other styles in varying proportions. We can also change our attachment style through therapy, mindfulness, and healing relationships. In doing so, we can develop what's known as an earned secure style. I personally began life with a highly anxious attachment style, which made any sign of threat to my primary attachments feel like a life-or-death situation. Only after years of therapy can I confidently say: If my partner can't meet my needs, I probably won't die. (That's what I like to call a very expensive sentence.)

While attachment theory is largely based on the nuclear family model, in which children are raised by one or two adult caregivers, other research has found that there are benefits to more community-centered models of child rearing. Research on

MY ATTACHMENT STYLE

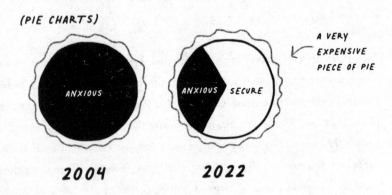

(PIE CHARTS)

ANXIOUS

ANXIOUS SECURE

A VERY
EXPENSIVE
PIECE OF PIE

2004   2022

attachment in Israeli, Dutch, and East African communities found that children with multiple primary caregivers, many of whom were members of their community of no blood relation, often experienced secure attachment to each parent figure and developed "more enhanced capacities to view the world from multiple perspectives." Our needs can be met in a variety of ways, and how they're met informs our psychology, physiology, and social behavior.

In order for an individual with an avoidant style to work toward a more secure style, they must gradually regain their awareness of the needs they've been repressing that did not previously feel safe to acknowledge. They must learn that it's safe to ask for help from others and even to depend on them. When people with an anxious style work toward secure attachment, they must learn that it's safe to relax their focus on others' behavior and to turn that attention inward. In doing so, they can grow their ability to soothe their own emotions and diversify their sources of support so they are not so dependent on their primary relationships.

People with disorganized styles will need to do a bit of each, and also work on developing a sense of internal safety in their own bodies and minds. They can benefit from trauma-informed care practices that help them feel safe expressing and enforcing boundaries with others, and growing relationships with safe people who will honor their needs and feelings. It's important to note that folks with secure attachments may also find themselves feeling more anxious, avoidant, or disorganized as adults depending on the relational experiences they have with adult partners.

Regardless of a person's attachment style, it takes time to feel comfortable depending on someone new. Most of us fall into group C at the beginning of a connection. It's healthy to gradually increase the needs we introduce to a relationship over time as trust grows. But sometimes we keep from asking for support even from those we're already close to because we fear it will jeopardize the relationship. We mistakenly assume that the perfect friend or partner never has needs. Trying to be needless actually keeps us from relaxing in a relationship, and keeps our connection from feeling balanced. When we're suffering, the people who love us want to help. When we refuse to let them, we're depriving them of the opportunity to feel useful to us. This can signal to them that we're not invested, or even that we're preparing to leave the relationship.

Reciprocal caregiving strengthens and stabilizes intimacy. A relationship in which both people get to ask for and receive help will have a healthier, more durable foundation. Rather than framing favors as a debt one must pay back, a balanced dynamic allows people to flow easily between give and take. In a truly mutualistic connection, both people will feel fulfilled whenever care is being exchanged. Helping others releases all three of the primary chemicals that contribute to happiness: oxytocin, dopamine, and serotonin. This is why some people talk about experiencing a "helper's high" after doing something caring or altruistic. When we let people help us, we're helping them, too.

HERE'S A LIST OF SOME COMMON RELATIONAL NEEDS:

EMOTIONAL SUPPORT

COMPANY

PHYSICAL TOUCH

REASSURANCE ABOUT
A CONNECTION

COMPLIMENTS

CONSTRUCTIVE CRITICISM

ADVICE ABOUT LIFE CHOICES

MONEY

ASSISTANCE WITH DAILY
TASKS

SPACE TO VENT

WHICH ARE EASIEST FOR YOU TO ASK FOR AND RECEIVE FROM OTHERS?
WHICH ARE HARDEST?

WHICH ARE EASIEST FOR YOU TO OFFER TO OTHERS? WHICH ARE HARDEST?

OUT OF BOUNDARIES

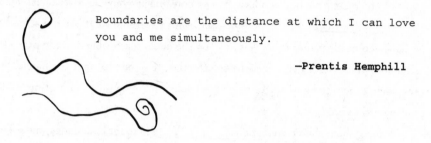

Boundaries are the distance at which I can love you and me simultaneously.

—Prentis Hemphill

WHENEVER I TALK ABOUT HOW WE SHOULD TAKE BETTER CARE OF EACH OTHER, I GET pushback from people who struggle with boundaries. They've seen the dangers of caring too much. They know how nightmarish relationships can become when one or both people can't say no. I understand their concern because I've seen it myself. Growing up, I watched my grandma give every ounce of her energy to her family. Three of her four kids have suffered through cycles of addiction, homelessness, and incarceration for most of their lives. And while some of those hardships were forced upon them by bad fortune and injustice, some of their struggles were the result of their own bad choices, many of which hurt other people as well

For years, I watched as my grandmother's health dwindled in the face of grueling stress and continuous efforts to save them. When one of them showed up in the middle of the night, she let them sleep on the couch. When someone needed bail, she always found the money. Then she'd sit in the dark, chain-smoking and rocking back and forth in misery. I felt heartbroken for her. I felt angry on her behalf. At some point, I started to feel angry at her. I gave her pep talks about how her needs mattered, too.

I tried to convince her that she could say no and that at some point, they had to live with the consequences of their decisions. Looking back, I have more empathy for the turmoil she must have been enduring. I can only imagine how devastating it would be to watch helplessly as your children suffer in such extreme ways. At the same time, it had become clear that there was nothing she could reasonably do to improve their situation. In order for her efforts to be effective, they had to want to change. Since they didn't seem to be willing or able to get sober, her help was only hurting her (and me, by extension).

Nothing about this conversation is simple. We need to set boundaries, and we need to help each other. Both are true. Part of why life on this planet is so messy is because our needs at times conflict. Negotiating that is not a perfect science, but it is a biological imperative. In relationships, we can't know in advance when or how we'll need to say no, but we can be sure that we'll need to. Without boundaries, our relationships become unsustainable. We give when we don't want to or can't afford to. We become resentful. In an effort to meet others' needs, we abandon our own. Maintaining our boundaries while remaining in connection requires self-awareness and communication.

I was introduced to the concept of boundaries when I was twenty years old. I was lucky enough to be exposed to Codependents Anonymous around that time. For those not familiar, Codependents Anonymous (or CoDA for short) is a support group formed in the 1980s as an extension of Alcoholics Anonymous. As a kid, I'd heard a lot of positive messages about AA because my grandparents had gotten sober through AA together. My grandma also felt grateful for twelve-step meetings because she knew that even when her kids had burned all their bridges, they could still always go to a meeting. CoDA focused not on those who abuse substances but on those in relationships with addicts, and the addictive nature that their connections often took on. People who identify as codependent may find themselves unable to function without access to their close connections, and saying no can feel almost impossible.

Over the years, CoDA expanded their definition from a focus on people married to alcoholics to anyone in a relationship they are unhealthily dependent on for emotional well-being. Much of the group's focus is on teaching members how to reclaim their sense of inner stability and confidence, often through the act of setting boundaries. These days, the collective discourse around boundaries has extended far beyond the reach of CoDA. Most therapists now espouse the necessity of boundaries in romantic, familial, and even professional relationships. But despite the ubiquity of these cultural conversations, many are still confused about what boundaries actually are and how they function.

Boundaries are an expression of a relational limitation. They are simply our way of saying what we can't or won't do. They can range in intensity from *I can't hang out Sunday* to *I quit*. Boundaries are healthy. They are not necessarily an indication of a relational problem. In fact, relationships are healthiest when they begin with frequent, clear expression of boundaries by all parties. Boundaries differ from ultimatums in that they are about us and our behavior, while ultimatums are demands we place on others. Here's an example of the difference:

A boundary sounds like: "I am leaving the party if you get drunk."

An ultimatum sounds like: "You cannot get drunk tonight or I'll leave you."

Learning to set boundaries is a process. At first, it can feel overwhelming. Whether you've just started saying no or need a refresher course, here are some simple ideas to remember.

TIPS FOR SETTING BOUNDARIES

Speak for Yourself. Your boundaries are always about you. They're not about teaching others a lesson, or trying to convince others to change. Boundaries are strictly about honoring your own capacity, limitations, and authentic desires. If you find yourself trying to slip a message about what others should do into your boundary setting, pause. Step back and reframe your boundary as a statement about yourself and your behavior.

Take Time Before Making Agreements. When someone makes a request of you, it's okay to take time before answering. The expression of needing time is in itself a boundary. First, make sure to get all the information you need to make an informed decision. Then pause and check in with yourself to see how you really feel. Imagine saying yes and then imagine saying no and notice the different sensations in your body that correspond with each answer. Investigate your motivations. Talk with others, if necessary, and respond when you're ready.

Observe Your Own Patterns. Make an effort to attend to your own emotional and behavioral patterns more closely. Reflect on what does and does not usually drain you. Keep track of how much you can typically do in a day before you start to feel exhausted. Knowing your own patterns will help you share them more clearly and reliably with others, and will help you know what to say no to.

Manage Your Resentment. If and when you end up saying yes to something you wish you'd said no to, notice the impact it has on how you feel. Notice how it changes your comfort level in that relationship. If you start to feel resentment, put yourself in a relationship time-out. You don't have to tell them you're doing this, but practice being more stringent for a while about what you do and don't want to share with this person. Resentment poisons relationships from the inside out. Only you know what you want and don't want, so only you can manage your own relational resentment.

OUT OF BOUNDARIES

Trust the Process. When you first start setting boundaries, it will likely feel very uncomfortable. You may need to overdo it for a while until you get the hang of it. This can look like declining an invitation when you're on the fence or saying no to new projects if you're even the slightest bit unsure of whether you have the capacity. This phase can be useful because it allows you to grow your no muscle and also gives the people in your life a chance to get used to your new practice (which they may be surprised, confused, or offended by at first). In time, you will likely grow more comfortable with setting boundaries, and the people in your life will grow more comfortable with receiving them. At that point, you can afford to be more flexible.

TIPS FOR HONORING OTHER PEOPLE'S BOUNDARIES

Boundaries are often about saying no, but they're also about accepting when others say no. A healthy boundary practice involves learning to regulate your response to other people's limitations and choices. Here are some tips for doing that:

Check In Before Hard Talks. Before bringing up a subject that may be difficult for you or your relational partner to discuss, check in about whether they have the capacity to discuss it right then. If the answer is no, don't keep talking about that subject. Try to transition to something else. If it feels right, ask them to let you know when they might be willing to discuss that issue with you in the future.

Try Not to Take No Personally. While it's easy to feel hurt when someone tells us no, a boundary is rarely an attack or insult. If anything, someone setting a boundary with us is a sign of trust. Other people's limitations often have nothing to do with us, but their willingness to tell us no may very well mean that they want to have an authentic relationship with us and they believe we want to know the truth of how they feel.

Regulate. If you're feeling confused or hurt after someone sets a boundary with you, try to call upon other sources of support. Go for a walk. Take a shower or hot bath. Call someone else you trust to discuss the issue. Distract yourself if necessary. Remember that respecting another person's boundaries is ultimately an act of love and will likely strengthen your relationship with them long-term.

Thank Them. When people tell us no, they're respecting themselves. If they intend to have a relationship with us in the future, their boundary may be the thing that's making it possible for our relationship to succeed. By managing their own resentment, they're actually being trustworthy. Even if it's less than fun to hear, we can thank them for their willingness to show up authentically in our connection.

Remember. If someone shares a boundary with you, try to remember it. If, for example, someone finds drug use triggering, try to put your drugs away before they come over. If someone hates phone calls and asks that you only call in an emergency, try to text beforehand asking if it's a good time to chat. Keeping track of the boundaries people share with us is a way of respecting the vulnerability they showed by trusting us with that knowledge in the first place.

Boundaries keep our relationships safe. They ensure that no one is being taken advantage of, and that no one is overextending themselves or sacrificing their safety for someone else's comfort. Boundaries are not a punishment or rejection, but a way of letting others know they can trust us to take care of ourselves without leaving the relationship. When boundaries are clear between people, we can feel confident that the connection is freely chosen and genuinely desired. The more easily we can say no, the more enthusiastically we can say yes.

As humans, we are in each other's keeping. Knowing how to balance our needs with the needs of others is more a dance than a decision. The issue of boundaries is complex because the dilemmas we face have to do with more than just our personal relationships. They're also influenced by the health of our communities. In a culture where so many people have unmet needs and so few people have a safety net, saying no can have dire consequences. In this context, highly empathetic people like my grandmother struggle even more to set boundaries because they know that they may be someone's last chance at survival. The more our society builds systems which ensure that everyone has their basic needs met, the easier it will be for each of us to set boundaries with one another.

We're all entitled to help, but not endlessly, and not from everyone. We each get to choose when and how to offer our support. A hyper-individualistic culture makes us believe that our needs have to be at odds, that either I get my way or you get yours. But with healthy boundaries, we can negotiate. We can cooperate. We can each take responsibility for ourselves while also taking care of one another.

COULDN'T SELF-CARE LESS

Rarely, if ever, are any of us healed in
isolation. Healing is an act of communion.

—bell hooks

IF YOU'VE MENTIONED TO ANYONE THAT YOU WERE FEELING STRESSED ABOUT ANYTHING in the last several years, you've probably been told to practice self-care. Stressed about work? Try yoga! Relationship problems? Make a gratitude list! Concerned about the downfall of society? Take a weekend away! Like any term that gets overused, it's lost some of its meaning. It's started to seem like self-care is anything that improves our well-being, but that's not really accurate. By definition, self-care is care that we, well, give ourselves. It's care we don't seek professional help to administer, at least not directly. Reading a book written by a mental health professional (you know, like the one you're currently reading) could qualify as self-care, but therapy does not. That's health care.

Self-care has become a buzzword for a reason. In addition to the fact that many of us take little time to show ourselves love, the self-care movement arose in response to an array of failures within the modern medical system. People are tired of being talked down to by health-care providers. They're sick of being prescribed mysterious medications by doctors who don't take the time to get to know them. They're also sick of being told what to do with their bodies. We all want to feel a sense of agency over our own well-being and to live a life we don't have to take painkillers to tolerate. The self-care industry promises to help us find that through individual empowerment, positive thinking, and messages about living our truth. This desire is valid. And as much as I understand why people are drawn to this movement, I have some concerns about where it's been heading.

When I talk about the self-care industry, I'm not talking about individual people practicing self-care. I'm talking about people building a brand by promoting things like yoga, chakra clearing, and other forms of "alternative" medicine. Don't get me wrong, I love yoga and chakra clearings. I'm not above any of this. It doesn't surprise me that people want an alternative to Western medicine. My issue with the self-care industry is not the practices themselves, but the ideas and tactics being used to sell them. For one thing, there's the issue of race and ethnicity. Many of the people getting paid to teach these often-indigenous practices are white, upper-class entrepreneurs who themselves hold thinly veiled racist and classist beliefs. There's something darkly twisted about a person getting rich by advocating for love and light while stealing the practices of a group of people that their ancestors either killed or impoverished.

The self-care industry exploits the shame we feel around being a burden. Relying on others is inherently vulnerable, and social messaging has added insult to that injury by implying that it's weak to be dependent and that taking care of yourself is the most dignified position. Glorifying self-care in an overly individualistic culture is dangerous because under capitalism, people have already been made to believe that their suffering is their own fault. They don't need to be told that they're responsible for their healing as well; they need to be told that it's okay to ask for help.

Self-care messaging reinforces the belief that we need to do "the work" on ourselves before we're ready to get into relationships. This just keeps us isolated. You can't prepare for relationships by being alone because relationships are largely how we grow and heal. Does this mean that our baggage sometimes impacts the people we're closest to? Yes. That's part of the deal. The self-care industry tries to convince us we can sidestep this, selling us methods of achieving inner peace that we can perform alone in the privacy of our own homes. This is not only misleading, it's ironic as the people telling you that you don't need anything from others are simultaneously trying to convince you that you need their products. That's because they need something from you, too: your money. Which they're getting. In 2020, people spent $120 billion on self-care related to mental health. While I'm glad folks in isolation had some source of solace, it saddens me to imagine people at their worst being sold the empty promise that something they purchase could bring real peace.

Many self-care gurus on Instagram and TikTok will tell you that all you have to do to achieve liberation is change your mindset. You have everything you need inside of you, they say. You choose your destiny, they say. (While cutting fresh mangoes in a rain forest hut that their dad paid the rent for.) There are kernels of truth in this message, as many of us do fail to acknowledge the power we have in life. But there are also limits to what we can influence. No matter who you are, there are aspects of your experience you can control and those that you can't. Any ideology that denies this is incomplete.

Many wellness influencers lack training in mental or physical health practices. In their lack of formal instruction, they sell customers themselves. Through indirect messaging, their branding seems to imply that you, too, can have a luxurious lifestyle if you think the right thoughts or develop the right attitude. This is convincing because as humans, we're notoriously bad at assessing cause and effect. We tend to assume that those who are wealthy and beautiful must have earned that status by being hardworking and virtuous. Partly, this has to do with the idea of the American Dream we've been sold: that anything is possible if you want it bad enough. Partly, though, it's a simple human error of cognition. If something good happens, we give ourselves credit for it. For this reason, people with immense social privilege may truly not recognize how much help they've received, and how much this factored into their favorable position. They may really think the "good attitude" they're trying to sell us is responsible for their riches.

When a person misattributes their own comfort to their work ethic, attitude, or other character strength, they automatically (and unconsciously) assume that others' lack of comfort is due to their lack of character. Another term for this is *victim blaming*, and it makes people feel more justified in denying others care. In this way, self-care rhetoric is often discriminatory against disenfranchised folks, including disabled people and survivors of abuse and oppression. It asserts that illness and hardship are a choice, and that if people really wanted to be well, they would be. Don't get me wrong, believing we're entirely in control of our destiny is tempting. It makes us feel powerful, which is a feeling many of us are desperate to experience. It also gives us permission to disengage from the messiness of politics as it frames the task of healing as a solitary, personal endeavor. This mission ultimately sets us up to fail, though. At some point, we inevitably find ourselves unable to resolve all our problems. Like toxic positivity, an overemphasis on self-care backfires, as it makes us all the more ashamed to own up to our struggles after indirectly accusing everyone else of causing their own.

Finally, self-care messages imply that wellness is simple. While it's a nice marketing strategy, anyone who says this is either mistaken or lying. Very few things in life are simple, and wellness is not one of them. Health, in its many facets, is a beautifully complex issue, shifting and fluctuating for each of us throughout our life based on a number of dynamic factors. Self-care is an important aspect of health—it's just not a solution. Self-care isn't a solution for poverty or chronic illness or the many ways oppression compromises mental health. In these cases, we need social and political change. Self-care practices can be beneficial and may even help us become a better partner or friend. But if they simply put a new spin on the individualistic thinking that's already tearing our communities apart, they're definitely not worth our money.

The truth is that we're not the masters of our own fate, at least not entirely. We do each have an incredible amount of power, and we are also subject to the laws of physics and the consequences of choices others make. If we're lucky enough to live to old age, we'll likely become just as reliant on the people we love as we were in infancy. This doesn't have to be a problem. True self-care comes from loving both our autonomy and our dependency, and accepting ourselves even at our most needy, which is to say, our most human.

ADULT BABYSITTER'S CLUB

A FEW YEARS AGO, I GOT A REALLY BAD FLU. IT CAME ON ABRUPTLY. MY EX AND I decided to take a nap and by the time we woke up I had a fever of 104. One thing about me is that I'm notorious for being very needy when I'm sick. Within an hour or two, I was full-on panicking, and he was getting full-on annoyed. He tried to calm me down with *The Office* and some Advil, but it wasn't working. The idea of getting stuck at his basement bachelor pad for what I could tell would be days of illness was harrowing. My grandma was high risk, so I knew I couldn't go stay with her. After a few minutes of chaotic deliberation, we decided to go to his parents' house.

Their home was a castle of comforts. I never once saw an item out of place in the multiple years we dated. It was not only immaculately decorated with items they'd collected while living in various countries across Asia, but it always had a well-stocked fridge and lots of clean blankets. While I didn't know his family that well yet, I knew them well enough to feel comfortable being there in my time of need. I still remember coming to my senses totally naked in their guest bed and looking up to see the kind face of his beautiful mother, water and medicine in hand. Even though I could sense that she was either confused, frustrated, or both, I knew I was safe. It took me almost two weeks to recover, during which time I didn't move a lot. More than once, I had to crawl to the bathroom in my underwear past his sister who already hated me. While these aren't my proudest moments, they did make great memories. (For them, not me.)

We all have times like these, when we just need someone nearby to comfort us. When we were kids, our parents hired slightly older kids to babysit us when they went out. Basically, all babysitters did was hang out in the next room in case anything went wrong. As adults, we also sometimes need this service. While we didn't call it that, I can think of so many times when friends have babysat me or I have done the sitting for them. After my grandma died, my best friend barely left my side for days. When my friend Ari contracted a debilitating illness from a mosquito, my friends and I made a spreadsheet of times each of us would bring him meals and read to him. For people from healthy cultures, this concept will seem silly to even state aloud. Of course we should take care of each other, a reasonable person is thinking. But for modern-day Americans, this idea can seem almost radical.

This isn't a new practice; it's actually how humans have survived for eons. A rise in solitary living has removed us from this simple, ancient form of support. We've become full of ourselves, thinking we can go through life without anyone cutting our food up for us. But when major life events occur, these small acts can be what help us make it through. The current thinking (in the States, at least) is that it's taboo to ask for help from most people unless we're paying them for it. But if we want to create a society where everything isn't controlled by five bald white guys, we need to normalize asking for and offering real, tangible support—for free. There are of course many things you can ask an adult babysitter to help you do, but here are some examples:

- *Make or bring food*
- *Run you a bath*
- *Help do your taxes or budget*

- *Hang out nearby when you're sad or sick*
- *Help with laundry or dishes*
- *Decorate or clean your house*
- *Sort through old photos or papers*
- *Watch movies or shows*
- *Tell you you're pretty*
- *Sleep in your guest room for a day or two*
- *Rub your shoulders*
- *Help you make hard phone calls*
- *Do (or wash) your hair*
- *Cuddle or take a nap*
- *Pick out clothes for an event*
- *Write a bio for a dating app*
- *Translate a document*
- *Pay your rent*
- *Write a résumé*
- *Edit your writing*

The reasons someone might need an adult babysitter are infinite. We go through illnesses, divorces, existential crises. Times when we just don't have it in us to adult. Social norms imply that we're not good company when we're depressed, so we try to wait until we feel better to get together with the people we love. But if isolation makes us feel even worse, that waiting can become a cycle. The lapse of communication since we last saw friends makes it more and more awkward to call, and suddenly it's been six months since we've spent quality time together. We don't have to do this.

It's completely healthy to ask a friend to be with you when you're depressed. Even if no words are exchanged, the simple act of sitting near each other can unlock certain levels of rest and restoration that are otherwise inaccessible. Co-regulating in this way helped our ancestors survive. And while there are benefits to the level of autonomy we've gained in the modern era, our nervous systems have suffered.

When you're the one babysitting, don't fuss too much about whether the other person is okay. Trust them to tell you. If they start crying, consider it a good thing. They'll stop at some point. Don't make critical comments about their emotional expressions, just enjoy that they feel comfortable enough to do things in your presence that they'd normally only do alone.

As we (re)learn to be with each other in a variety of states, we realize that every one of us is a whole-ass person with flaws and quirks and strange ways of soothing ourselves. Being alive is embarrassing—there's no way around it. Being born is embarrassing, getting sick is embarrassing, falling in love is the most embarrassing thing ever. There's no way to avoid embarrassment, so we may as well embrace it. We may as well stop being so precious with ourselves and admit that we're not the exception. We're just like everybody else, fucked up and lonely and susceptible to the flu. By letting others keep us company when we're at our worst, we give them permission to do the same, to show up just as they are.

NOT EVERYBODY'S CUP OF TEA PARTY

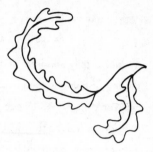

Nothing I accept about myself can be used
against me.

—Audre Lorde

EVERYONE CARES WHAT PEOPLE THINK. YES, EVEN YOU. AS SOCIAL CREATURES, WE'RE wired to care what people think. In moderation, this is healthy. For much of human history, our survival depended on being accepted by a group. If a whole community hated someone, they might have been sent to live in the woods alone. This often resulted in being eaten by bears. Even today, in our less bear-filled world, reputation matters. We need each other to survive, and we need to feel a sense of belonging to be well. So while the idea of not caring what anyone thinks might sound cool, it's actually not a great goal.

That said, how we go about seeking belonging matters greatly. Defining ourselves entirely by what others think obviously isn't healthy either. In her book *The Gifts of Imperfection*, Brené Brown talks about the difference between belonging and fitting in, saying that fitting in is actually "the greatest barrier to belonging." Real belonging asks us to stay true to ourselves, while fitting in often means changing who we are to gain false approval. Belonging can happen only if we're authentic. When we're authentic, some people inevitably won't like us. That's just the way the cookie crumbles.

Being disliked is not necessarily a sign that we've done anything wrong. No one is universally admired, and trying to be is very exhausting. Learning to tolerate the feeling of being judged is part of loving ourselves. No matter who you are, some people won't enjoy you. Maybe they'll disagree with your worldview. Maybe they'll find you boring. Maybe they just won't like your face. (Not me, I think your face is great.) I have personally been disliked by lots of people. Did I let it bring me down? Absolutely. Did I cry about it? Yes, many times. But did I let it stop me from being myself? No, because after careful consideration, I decided that I disagree with my haters. (Mostly. Some of y'all made some pretty good points, though.)

Over the years, I've come to appreciate critical feedback. It helps me see myself from a new angle. At the end of the day, I get to choose whether to take someone's feedback into consideration. On some occasions, learning why a person doesn't like me has made me like myself more. For example, some folks describe me as rude, uncouth. I'm not much for decorum, and I tend to lie down on the floor whenever I'm tired. I totally get why someone might think that's obnoxious. People have the right to their opinion, just as I have a right to lie down on the floor of TJ Maxx. Being judged is a part of life.

Like it or not, people have the right to reject us just as we have the right to reject them. Being disliked and misunderstood can be a great opportunity for self-reflection. When someone criticizes us, it's important to remember that there are lots of reasons why this could be. For starters, they are a different person with a totally different psychology. Their opinion could be based on bias or an experience that has nothing to do with us. They could also be seeing something about us that we don't see yet. In that case, we can be grateful. Determining which of these is the case isn't easy. It can take some serious self-reflection (and help from trusted others). Once we make sense of why we're not someone's favorite person, we can decide whether we want to work on that or learn to let their judgments go. Either way, we gain awareness. In order to find this clarity, however, we'll have to take a hard look at ourselves. Why not do it with tea?

WHO

Hosting a Not Everybody's Cup of Tea Party is both a great way to deepen your friendships and also just a lovely way to spend an afternoon. This event will work best with a tight, intimate crowd. Ideally, four to eight people. This event is for you and people who already like you. If someone doesn't already possess a general fondness for who you are, they are not the people whose opinion you're seeking here. Don't invite any frenemies. In fact, before inviting someone to this party, you may want to confirm that they actually do like you. You should like them also!

WHEN

Once you've compiled a list of mutual admirers, choose an afternoon when you all have a good two to three hours free. If possible, pick a day when you have nowhere to rush to afterward. You may need a nap.

WHAT

I'm serious about the tea. It's soothing, fun, and it comes in little boxes that you'll need for the activity. You'll also need mugs (duh) as well as paper, pens, and tissues. Before your guests arrive, make sure you have a variety of beverage options: caffeinated and herbal, sweet and earthy. Ask others to bring their favorites. Cut some lemon wedges, set out honey and oat milk. Maybe buy a tin of cookies, I don't know. Blankets should be stocked. The more comfy, the less likely that someone will get super upset, so create a soothing setting.

You'll also want to prep feedback boxes beforehand or at the beginning. For each person present, you need a small box—empty tea boxes work. Put their name on that box and decorate it if you're feeling festive. Then set it on a counter somewhere so everyone can add their notes.

HOW

Start by getting cozy. Drink tea and chat for a bit. At some point, call the group to attention. Explain the premise of the event. (Optional script below.) If people are nervous, allow them to ask questions up front. Let everyone know the agenda. Reassure the group that this is a space of love and respect.

Opening script:

We're gathered here today to learn to love ourselves more. By embracing that no one is everybody's cup of tea, we deepen our practice of self-acceptance. Sometimes people see things in us that we ourselves can't see yet. Determining when and if we want to learn from that feedback is part of the process of growing up. There's no greater dignity than loving ourselves in the midst of transformation. We're everchanging, ever-evolving, and each stage is worth honoring. As friends, we're here to help each other sort through the muck to find the gems of feedback we can use to morph into our next stage of being.

Write feedback. Set a timer for fifteen minutes. Let everyone know that there's no talking during this portion, so you can focus on forming your thoughts. Turn on some music and give everyone time to write out their feedback before placing it into each person's feedback box. Notes will ideally be anonymous, although it may be obvious who wrote what if your group is small.

Remember, these are your friends. You like them! Feedback should not be mean. It should absolutely not be related to things a person can't control, like their physical appearance, social class, sexuality, etc. It should feel like a genuine offering of perspective. There's a big difference between helping someone see a blind spot and flat-out criticism. Make sure to express yourself from a place of respect and affection. It helps to remember that others are the way they are for a reason. When we give people the benefit of the doubt, it comes through in our language. Here are some examples of productive and unproductive ways of wording feedback.

SAY THIS, NOT THIS:

Unproductive: "You're loud and annoying."
Productive: "You have a big personality that can overpower those who are more reserved."

Unproductive: "You're boring. You never have anything interesting to say."
Productive: "It can be hard to tell what you're excited about."

Unproductive: "You're mean. You make everyone feel bad about themselves."
Productive: "Sometimes your tone can be harsh."

OTHER FEEDBACK IDEAS:

"You can come across as aloof when you're uncomfortable."

"Your anxiety can be contagious, and in those moments it's hard to know how to soothe you."

"There are times when I feel like you're distracted or not really hearing me."

"Your assertiveness can make it seem like you're not open to working with others to find a win-win solution."

"I sometimes wonder if you'll follow through with plans."

"At times, it feels like your mood changes suddenly, and I'm not always sure why."

Notice how words like "sometimes" soften feedback because they show that we understand that the other person isn't always this way, only some of the time. Expressing an awareness of what you see that a person is trying to do also helps them see we're giving them the benefit of the doubt, and we know they're not intentionally being difficult. Last, speaking in the first person helps them hear that we're not stating anything as fact, just sharing a possible perception.

Once the timer goes off, circle up again. Pass each person their box, then take about five minutes to look through the notes quietly. Once everyone's had a chance to read their notes, it's time for show and tell!

Share. Like everything else in this book, sharing is optional. No one should be forced to read what their feedback says aloud. It can be very helpful, though, to offer space for folks to talk through what they received and how they're feeling about it. Let people speak popcorn style. Take turns going around the circle talking about what your feedback said, how it makes you feel initially, and whether or not you see that in yourself. This is a great time to ask for clarity if you don't understand what something means. You can also ask for reassurance, of course.

Sort Your Feedback. Turn the music back up and give folks some time to organize their feedback into groups:

If you decide that you agree with the feedback, or you can see how someone would feel that way, place it in the agree pile. If you think it's a misunderstanding of who you are, place it in the disagree pile.

Once you've sorted your notes into those two piles, sort them further. If you agree with something, decide whether you want to work on it or if you like that about yourself and are okay with others disliking it. If you disagree, determine whether you want to work on it by trying to make a different impression in those cases or if you want to practice accepting that sometimes people misunderstand you.

Describe Your Plan. Circle up one more time and share what you plan to work on and what you plan to let go. You can offer to help each other commit to your pursuit of working on these things or letting them go. It can be helpful to have the support and accountability of others. Below are some tools that may assist you in your process of working on something or letting it go.

PRACTICES FOR WORKING ON IT

Find a great therapist.

Read books about the issue you want to work on.

Engage in regular accountability check-ins with friends.

Join a support group with others who are working on themselves.

PRACTICES FOR LETTING IT GO

Develop a meditation practice.

Spend more time in nature.

Find or return to a creative practice.

Make and repeat daily affirmations.

Journal Prompts for Working on Yourself

WHAT ASPECTS OF THIS BEHAVIOR HAVE I NOT PREVIOUSLY NOTICED?

WHAT EFFECT MIGHT THIS BEHAVIOR HAVE HAD ON OTHERS?

WHAT DO I FEEL WHEN I THINK ABOUT HAVING MISSED THIS INFORMATION?

ARE THERE ANY PEOPLE IN PARTICULAR WHOM I FEEL THIS PART OF ME HAS NEGATIVELY IMPACTED?

HOW MIGHT I MAKE AMENDS?

HOW MIGHT I INCREASE MY EMPATHY FOR OTHERS WHO HAVE EXPERIENCED THIS BEHAVIOR OF MINE?

HOW MIGHT I INCREASE MY EMPATHY FOR THIS PART OF MYSELF?

Journal Prompts for Letting It Go

WHAT ASSUMPTIONS MAY OTHERS HAVE MADE ABOUT ME THAT ARE INCORRECT?

WHAT DO I WISH THEY SAW IN ME INSTEAD?

WHAT DO I FEEL WHEN I THINK ABOUT BEING INCORRECTLY PERCEIVED IN THIS WAY?

HOW MIGHT I INCREASE MY EMPATHY FOR THOSE MISPERCEIVING ME?

HOW MIGHT I INCREASE MY EMPATHY FOR THIS PART OF MYSELF?

TO DON'T LIST

WE SPEND A LOT OF TIME THINKING ABOUT WHAT WE WANT TO DO. WHAT IF WE SPENT some of that time thinking about what we don't want to do? As the self-improvement movement threatens to all but consume us, it's important to sometimes let things be good enough. A To Don't list is a simple practice for saying no. Here's mine.

THIS YEAR, I WILL <u>NOT</u>:

lose weight
become less clingy
remodel my house
get rich
work on my brand
become enlightened
learn to play the cello
get over my ex
become fluent in spanish (or any other
language that I don't already speak)

WHAT GOALS HAVE YOU BEEN CONSIDERING PURSUING FOR SIX MONTHS OR
LONGER THAT YOU HAVEN'T GOTTEN STARTED ON?

HOW MIGHT IT FEEL TO LET THAT GOAL GO FOR NOW?

ARE THERE ANY ASPIRATIONS YOU HOLD THAT FEEL MORE TIED TO
EXTERNAL PRESSURE THAN GENUINE INTEREST?

WHAT COMMITMENTS WOULD YOU LET GO OF IF YOU TOOK ON ONLY WHAT
YOU REALLY WANTED TO DO?

WHAT MISERY LOVES

THE NEED
FOR SOCIAL HEALING

KNOW YOUR RITES

WHEN I WAS A KID, I WAS OBSESSED WITH OUIJA BOARDS. THERE WASN'T MUCH religion in my house, so it genuinely didn't occur to me that rallying a group of seven-year-old girls from Nebraska to make contact with dead movie stars would ruffle feathers. Despite the parental backlash that followed, I felt something when we put our hands together on the planchette that I hadn't felt before. Despite my lack of familiarity with church, I also felt it when I joined my friends at Mass and, later, while holding signs next to thousands of strangers at protests. It wasn't the Ouija board or even the possibility of hearing from Selena that sparked my interest, but the ritual of it, the way that joining with others in a united cause blurred the edges between us and made things seem possible.

"Ritual" can be a contentious word. Some think it means witches dancing naked around a fire. And while that is what I personally mean by ritual, many other, more common activities are rituals, too, like lighting candles for church service, reciting wedding vows, buying presents at Christmas, or even making coffee every morning. Like these, many commonplace cultural traditions are actually rituals. Rituals have been a central feature of every human culture since the dawn of mankind. Some scholars even go so far as to argue that rituals are what make us human. But as our rituals vary so much from person to person and culture to culture, you may be wondering what actually makes a ritual a ritual.

A ritual is any set of actions performed in a predetermined order and repeated over time. Some rituals are religious, while others have more to do with getting through daily life. Rituals can center around everything from physical milestones, to changes in season and political events. Some rituals, like funerals, are intended to help us cope with loss. Others, like weddings or graduations, allow us to understand a new or changing role in our communities. Rituals differ from habits in the sense that they must be understood to hold meaning. Without meaning, for example, "the 21-gun salute during a military funeral service, rather than bestowing the highest honor to a fallen comrade, would be nothing more than a group of soldiers firing into the air." This is true about many of our most sacred cultural rituals. Part of the power of a ritual lies in the fact that each time we participate in it, the steps are the same. These actions are done in an attempt to achieve a symbolic state of internal change, rather than as a way of accomplishing a more overt or tangible goal.

Despite their ubiquity, the modern attitude toward ritual can be skeptical, even antagonistic. For many, the concept conjures images of occult behavior and ancient, now illegal practices. While there are certainly rituals that have gone out of style for good reason, many others were lost due to religious persecution, genocide, and forced assimilation into colonial cultures. Humans the world over have always used ritual to cope with change, release strong emotions, and maintain connection to community.

Ritual can help us make sense of minor and major events, and provide insight into the broader meaning of our lives. Without it, we can feel disoriented, dislocated, and without direction. Writer Ken Kesey put it this way: "Ritual is necessary for us to know anything." When we lack ritual to understand the things that happen, our lives move forward without our full acknowledgment of what's taken place. We can feel stuck in the past, unable to get back to the present. Many of us experienced this during the quarantine era of COVID, when our inability to perform our typical routines contributed to a feeling of confusion about where we were in time and space.

Whether we know it or not, most of us practice rituals of some kind, but we often do so sheepishly, unconsciously, or drunkenly. It's like we sense that we should do something to mark significant events, but we feel embarrassed to be making a big deal out of anything. This causes our rituals to lose their power. From a mental health perspective, it keeps us from experiencing the well-documented benefits of ritual, which include coping with uncertainty and failure, regulating emotions, setting and reaching goals, and feeling more confident. Rituals also help alleviate anxiety, mitigate grief, and provide a sense of control over one's experience.

As it turns out, you don't actually have to believe in the meaning behind a ritual to experience the benefits. Even an entirely arbitrary set of actions has been shown to enhance focus and self-esteem, as long as participants stick to the steps. This was demonstrated in the 2016 study where researchers asked karaoke performers to draw a picture, sprinkle salt on it, count backward, and then throw it away. After completing the ritual, their singing accuracy improved by 13 percent. Sometimes the meaning does matter, though. Depending on one's spiritual or religious beliefs, rituals can provide an opportunity to feel connected with a higher power or the universe at large. Whether or not a person is spiritual, rituals can induce a state known as "flow," which is characterized by feelings of ecstasy, lack of self-consciousness, and full immersion in what one is doing. Flow can feel to some like a transcendent, spiritual state, and has been shown to produce long-lasting mental health benefits, even being dubbed by some as the "secret to happiness."

Ritual can give our tired brains a break by allowing for a different kind of thinking. Psychologists refer to this as bottom-up processing. As opposed to its counterpart top-down processing, bottom-up processing occurs when we "build perceptions based on sensory information." It's what happens when we go for a long walk outside and allow our minds to wander. The environment itself informs our thinking, as opposed to our typical style of thinking in the modern day, when we use previously acquired knowledge to analyze what's happening. Both are necessary, but our current lifestyles often place an emphasis on top-down thinking, which contributes to mental fatigue. Ritual can help.

Rituals, when done well, create an energetic container for the safe release of emotion, an important form of catharsis that's become socially taboo. The opportunity to lose oneself in the company of others, and to express the full force of a feeling in an uninhibited way, produces immense psychological benefit. While rituals practiced alone can be extremely healing, rituals practiced with others offer additional advantages. For one, group rituals are a powerful way to quickly and reliably establish bonds, and have historically also been used to maintain a sense of belonging within a community. We know that our brain waves mimic those we spend the most time with, but studies have also shown a remarkable physiological alignment among individuals who don't know one another and who are participating in a group ritual. It seems that even just observing a ritual can bring about this form of connection. During a fire-walking ceremony in Spain, scientists observed that the heart rates of spectators synced with those of the firewalkers themselves with astonishing precision.

Participation in group rituals has been known to produce a state called collective effervescence. *Collective effervescence* (CE for short) is experienced by large groups of people who are so fully engaged in some kind of ritual that a sense of electricity is formed between them. Think concerts and sporting events. CE is akin to an altered state, a feeling of transcendence that "transports the individuals into a new, ideal realm, lifts them up outside of themselves, and makes them feel as if they are in contact with an extraordinary energy." Humans have been engaging in these large-scale group rituals for most of our history, likely seeking that feeling.

Author and pagan educator Starhawk is no stranger to the power of group ritual. She has widely discussed the benefits of social ceremony, but also cautions us to respect their power: "Ritual is an opportunity for transformation. If you aren't willing to be changed by the ritual, don't do it." In one sense, ritual is an opportunity to be transformed. In another, it's a way of processing transformation that has already taken place. Both acts can occur simultaneously. Without ritual, it's not that we never change, it's just that we may not know how we've changed or feel able to put those changes into practice.

As a species, we have always mourned together. When we don't, grief doesn't truly metabolize in a community. Grieving helps us feel that the trauma is over. Without a collective grief practice, we may feel stuck in a dreamlike state, unaware of whether a threat has passed or a loss has really occurred. This unprocessed grief festers. It can manifest in the form of distrust of each other and chronic social unrest. In the United States, we see this backlog of grief spilling over, from high-energy protests to labor strikes to massive upticks in mental illness. With so much to grieve and so few proper grief practices to turn to, we can easily become hopeless and weighed down.

Of course, rituals have their dark side as well. Just as rituals can help us feel like part of a group, they can also embolden us in judging those outside of our group. Behavioral researcher Michael Norton has found that even participating in a simple ritual that he informs the audience he invented can still become a source of in-group and out-group exclusion. In just a couple minutes of teaching one another the steps, people begin judging those who make mistakes (say, clapping when they were told to stomp). This is how powerful ritual is as a social bonding tool. Even when we know it's made up, we implicitly put stock into the rules.

While many crave this sense of ceremony and communion with others, some of us aren't sure how or where to find such opportunities. For those who don't identify with a religion, or whose religion is unpopular in their region, finding others with whom to practice ritual can be very difficult. For those of us who are queer, nonmonogamous, or otherwise at odds with the dominant culture we exist within, it can feel like ritual isn't available. In some cases, the only opportunity we have to participate in meaningful group activities is by frequenting drunken dance floors, places where we may feel unsafe for other reasons.

Before engaging in a specific ritual, it's important to ask ourselves where the practice came from. What community developed it? How might our participation affect that community? There is no one right answer, but curiosity and caution are warranted. Sometimes the answer is that certain practices aren't for us. That's okay. Chances are, there's another tradition we can participate in. In order to find which rituals work for us, we may all have to do some research into our ancestry and rediscover traditions tied to our cultural heritage. If those aren't available to us or don't serve our needs well, we can draw from modern innovations and universal practices to design our own rituals. Ritual is for everyone.

WHAT RITUALS OR CEREMONIES, IF ANY, DID YOU GROW UP PRACTICING? HOW DID YOU FEEL ABOUT THEM?

WHAT RITUALS OR TRADITIONS DO YOU KNOW OF THAT EXIST WITHIN YOUR SPIRITUAL OR ETHNIC LINEAGE? IF YOU DON'T KNOW MUCH ABOUT YOUR SPIRITUAL OR ETHNIC ANCESTRY, HOW MIGHT YOU COME TO BETTER UNDERSTAND THE TRADITIONS TIED TO THEM?

WHAT EVENTS IN YOUR LIFE DO YOU THINK RITUAL MIGHT HELP YOU PROCESS?

MOMENT SAUCE

Rituals are most powerful when practiced in environments that stimulate our senses. Environment greatly affects our mood, and since ritual is all about achieving certain moods, the setting is all the more important. Bottom-up processing relies on incoming sensory information to formulate perception. In ritual, we're trying to attain transcendent states, and our ritual space can either inhibit that goal or help us achieve it. Everything from the sounds and sights in a room to the temperature of the air will influence how we feel there. With some conscious tweaking, we can create the right vibe. My friend Erik calls this the "moment sauce."

Anything external we set up to enhance our enjoyment of a moment could be called moment sauce: good speakers, incense, mood lighting. These features inarguably alter our experience, and can create an environment that reinforces the theme or emotion our ritual centers around. For a somber tone, we may want a dark, quiet setting. To encourage relaxation, we may want to create a cozy space, with lots of soft blankets around and comfortable places to rest. No matter what mood we're aiming for, our space should smell good. Below is a list of potential ingredients you can use to find your moment sauce style.

MOMENT SAUCE RECIPE

Sight: Dimming the lights is usually a good idea. I keep a red lightbulb in one of my lamps at all times because turning it on instantly creates a sensual, uninhibited effect. I also love twinkle lights. Art can create infinite moods. Consider hanging some art around your space. Whenever you can afford to, support local artists!

Smell: Incense, candles, flowers, oils, or dried herbs either burned or arranged as part of a centerpiece. A simmer pot of orange peels, cinnamon sticks, and cloves is a favorite of mine. Fresh air is usually a good idea, too, but even fans circulating indoor air can help maintain a pleasant aroma.

Sound: Good music is essential. These days, there are many ways to create playlists and play music, but remember to keep the volume low enough that folks can still hear one another. If and when it's time to turn the music up, invest in a solid speaker system!

Taste: It's never a bad idea to include something for guests to drink and eat. I always try to have something with caffeine and something without, as well as something with alcohol and something without. Fruits (fresh or dried), a variety of nuts, and vegan chocolate are often good snacks because most people can eat them, regardless of dietary restrictions.

Touch: Include blankets, no matter what time of year. Make sure floors and surfaces are clean so people can spread out comfortably. Keep the temperature between sixty-eight and seventy-two degrees Fahrenheit, if you can control it.

LOSE IT CREW

I'VE ALWAYS MADE FRIENDS EASILY. MAYBE IT'S BECAUSE I'M AN ONLY CHILD, SO LEARN-ing to socialize was essential. Maybe it's because I'm extroverted, or naturally a people person, or because I have a lot of interests. Who knows, who cares. I know that not everyone is naturally a social butterfly, and also that much of what I'm proposing in this book requires that you have at least a couple close connections. If you're not someone who mingles easily, fear not. You can still find your people. I don't want you to find just anybody, either. I want you to meet people you can really go deep with, share your most humiliating thoughts and feelings with, look like absolute trash and still feel loved and accepted with. Really just lose it with these folks. Here are some tips for finding them.

Make a List of the Things You Like to Do with Others. What do you love to do alone but haven't been able to share with anyone else yet? What have you enjoyed doing with friends in the past? What activities feel most natural and rewarding to you? Write them down. Try to get specific: the more clearly you define an activity, the easier it will be to find others who like to do that thing the way you do. Here's mine:

Dance: Specifically to pop and rock music, but not just in a drunken way. Extra points if singing is also involved. Extra extra points if costumes are involved.

Talk: About psychology, philosophy, social justice, literature, and relationships. In the right company, I could talk for days. For some people, this would be a nightmare. These people are not in my Lose It Crew.

Trade Massages: Enough said.

Hike: Or rather, go for laid-back walks in wild places.

Go to Art Museums: Or bookstores. Or record stores. Or concerts. Bonus points for friends who like to linger without necessarily buying anything.

Figure Out Where People Are Doing These Things and Go There: Google "dance events near me" or whatever your interest is.

Get Online: In an effort to avoid making this book sound dated in two years, I won't list the specific apps I use, but I'm sure there will be social apps when you read this. I've made some incredible friends online. It feels much less cringey to me than online dating. Whether it's an interest-based online group or a dating app that has a friend-making feature, there are lots of people online looking to meet people for platonic relationships.

Now, before you get on there and set up a profile, let's talk about bios. I know that a lot of people hate writing bios, but please, for the love of all that is good and holy, take two seconds to actually write something if you're trying to meet people. As a writer, I'm a bit of a snob about this, but it shocks me how many people write nothing in their profile, or write statements that mean nothing. Below are some sentences to avoid because they give people zero information about who you are.

- *I'm looking to meet people*—right. We all are. That's . . . why we're here.
- *I like to have fun*—again, who doesn't? Tell me what your idea of fun is.
- *I'm nice unless someone upsets me!*—I read this as a sort of veiled threat, but I'm not sure it does what people think it does. Someone is not going to read that and decide to treat you well if they weren't planning to already.

Try these ideas instead:

- If you're into personality theory, list your test results. My favorites are the Enneagram and the MBTI. I can tell a lot about a person by reading these.
- Astrological signs, of course.
- List three of your interests. Be as specific as possible. Try this formula: *I like to [verb + noun]. (E.g., ride horses, play video games, fix bikes.)*
- Now list three adjectives other people have used to describe you: *I'm intense, outgoing, and creative.*
- Last, list one thing that has happened to you that's strange or unique: *I once got stuck overnight in rural Canada in a town where Elton John happened to be performing, so there was only one hotel with vacancies nearby, and it was extremely expensive and also terrifying. In the morning, the continental breakfast was a bunch of Eggo waffles that looked and smelled like plastic stacked tightly inside a dirty storage bin; the waffles were set out on a wooden conference table in a room with high pile carpet and no windows. I haven't eaten a waffle since.*

Practice Opening Up. You've made some friend dates. You're meeting people you share interests with. You're going to do stuff you both like to do. Then what?! For those who struggle to open up with new people, here's a theory that may be helpful.

Social penetration theory was developed by psychologists Irwin Altman and Dalmas Taylor to demystify the process by which two people get to know each other. In this theory, they used the metaphor of an onion to describe the layers of self-disclosure that happen naturally when two people are bonding. For those who are reserved, it can be helpful to know that moving through these zones of sharing is a tried-and-true equation for getting closer to someone. It's a bit like a cheat sheet for making friends.

- Acquaintance: *Small talk. What's your name, etc.*
- Casual Connection: *Starting to reveal more authentic aspects of self.*
- New Friend: *Making plans. Sharing your unique perspective.*
- Close Friends: *Talking about your deeply held values and regularly asking for help.*
- Best Friends: *Exploring future goals together. Helping each other overcome fears and achieve dreams.*
- Family: *Feeling understood and accepted as you are.*

One thing to remember is that self-disclosure should be mutual. If you share multiple vulnerable pieces of information about yourself and the person does not reciprocate, this may be a sign that they're not available for an emotionally connective relationship. Do yourself a favor and stop sharing until they demonstrate an interest and ability to match your level of engagement.

When you don't know what to say, you can always ask questions. People typically love to talk about themselves, especially to someone who seems interested. Here are some *fun and light* questions to try asking folks at your next social gathering.

SELF DISCLOSURE ONION

Do you believe in past lives?

What creature would you like to trade bodies with for an hour?

What's your favorite shade of purple?

Who was the first person you felt understood by?

Would you rather go to the bottom of the ocean or space?

What meal would you eat even if you were full?

A NOTE ON TRAUMA BONDING

I want to quickly address the subject of trauma bonding, as people ask me about it often. I find that my clients and those around me feel afraid to connect with others over painful emotions or events out of fear that doing so is unhealthy and will mean that they form a so-called trauma bond. This fear, though, comes from a misunderstanding of the term. For those who aren't familiar, a trauma bond occurs when we develop an unhealthy attachment to someone who abuses us or someone we have a mutually abusive relationship with. Trauma bonds can intensify as more abuse occurs. As the abuse increases, so does the shame, leading the people in the relationship to feel that they can't talk about what happens between them with anyone else because nobody else would relate. When the abuse is unilateral, this feeling is often manipulated by the abuser to keep the other person from talking about it.

Contrary to popular belief, a trauma bond is not a relationship with someone you lived through a trauma with, or with whom you share a similar history. That's just a bond. If your life has involved a lot of trauma, bonding will involve talking about that. It concerns me when I hear people questioning their friendships because they met through mutual hardship, got closer after the death of a loved one, or overcame some other challenge together. Just because certain relationships formed out of struggle doesn't mean they're not positive connections! You don't need to feel guilty for bonding with people based on shared experiences. That is human nature, and it's healthy. Now, if your trauma is the only thing you talk about with this person, that's worth looking at. But then again, it's also not great if the only thing you can talk to someone about is knitting or baseball. Healthy relationships involve a broad, dynamic set of conversational topics.

If you're worried that you might be involved in an actual trauma bond, please seek professional help right away. If you sense that you're in a relationship that simply centers too much around pain, let the other person know that. Express your desire to open up a more diverse set of talking points between you. If your connection is healthy, the other person may be hurt, but they'll also understand and will want to work with you to discover other ways you can connect.

TRUST ISSUES

> To be trusted is a greater compliment than being loved.
>
> **—George MacDonald**

WHENEVER I START WORK WITH A NEW CLIENT, I TRY TO REMEMBER THAT I'M A stranger to them. They don't know anything about my history, the books I've read, or my ethical beliefs. They don't know that I'm the kind of person who compulsively hangs things back up at thrift stores even when I'm not the one who messed them up, and I don't expect them to. I understand that, to them, I'm just a lady with a lot of tattoos and weird art on my walls. Just because I have letters after my name doesn't mean they know they can trust me. Now, therapy is obviously an exceptional circumstance. It's not often that a person is expected to divulge information about the most difficult aspects of their experience within minutes of meeting. But while the therapeutic process asks for more trust more quickly, all connections require trust.

Trust is always a risk, especially at first. When someone is trying to decide whether they can trust us, they're trying to assess whether it's safe to be vulnerable with us. They're asking themselves questions like: "Will they judge me?" "Will they take advantage of what I share?" "Will they suddenly disappear as soon as I start to depend on them?" The more quickly and effectively we can put these fears to rest, the more trust we'll earn.

Building trust is an active process. It doesn't just happen on its own. It requires participation from each person, both in the offering of information (and behavior to back it up) as well as the willingness to assume the best about the other person before we have much proof of who they are. The most common mistake people make in trying to build trust with others is assuming that good intentions are enough. Other people don't know what's in our hearts and minds. We have to show them. And we have to do it in a way that makes sense to them, which means we have to learn about them and their past as we go.

We all have complex histories and identities. We have pain we want to avoid experiencing again and ways we prefer to be treated. It takes time to reveal these parts of ourselves and to learn about others. The more we get to know someone, the more we can use the knowledge we gain to customize how we treat them. In every group of friends, you'll find people with a huge array of backgrounds that affect what makes them feel safe. In my friend group, I know that Gina gets overwhelmed easily, so I don't pressure her to come out if she's had a long week. I know that Mary gets really lonely, so I make sure to invite her to arrive early to events if I can. I know that Greg had an abusive father, so I try not to get too loud around him. Each of these considerations is the result of months if not years of active trust-building between us.

All of this requires effort, and it can be exhausting. The good news is that people want to trust. Nobody wants to walk around feeling suspicious of others. When we make it possible for people to trust us, we give them a gift. We allow them to put their guard down, which most people will do as soon as they feel they safely can.

Even once some safety has been established, trust is rarely an all-or-nothing issue. Rather than asking, "Can I trust this person?," we're better off asking, "What can I trust this person to do?" As my old therapist told me the thirty-seventh time I asked whether she thought I could trust my partner: "No one is entirely trustworthy. We are all safe in some ways and unsafe in others." Our expectations of one another must reflect this nuance. Trust is a matter of both kind and degree. Some people can be trusted to be supportive but not punctual, or helpful but not gentle. The clearer our expectations are within a relationship, the more easily trust can grow.

Being part of a social species is strange because it means that other people are the ultimate source of safety and also the ultimate danger. As humans, we are remarkably vulnerable to one another. The amount of pain we can cause each other is profound, as is the joy we can bring. Despite this sticky situation, we all have to practice trusting. So how do we decide with whom to take that risk? Here are some questions to ask yourself when considering whether to trust a new person.

- *Are they consistent? Are their words and actions aligned? If there's a contradiction, do they notice and acknowledge it?*
- *Are they self-aware? Do they seem to know what they want in life and relationships? Do they know what their strengths and weaknesses are?*
- *Are they open? Do they seem curious about other people's experience? Are they willing to learn from feedback?*
- *Do they communicate? Are they willing and able to share their thoughts and feelings? Do they ask about yours (and listen to your answer)?*

When you're trying to assess whether someone is safe enough to get close to, turn to your body for insight. Notice how you feel physically before, during, and after spending time with them. Do you get an upset stomach every time you hang out? Do you feel tired when you see them and energized when you leave? Notice these patterns, and take stock of what they might mean.

The reason trusting others is so scary is because it creates the potential for betrayal.

Betrayal can be life-altering. It can cause us to question whether anyone is safe, or whether we'll know how to keep from being betrayed again. Learning to trust is not about guaranteeing that we'll never get hurt. It's about recognizing that getting hurt isn't a failure. In order to show up fully in relationships, we have to surrender to the inherent danger involved. We have to trust ourselves enough to know we can survive it if we do get hurt. Connection is what happens when we trust ourselves together, and that is worth the risk.

WHAT IS YOUR RELATIONSHIP WITH TRUST? DO YOU SEE YOURSELF AS SOMEONE WHO TRUSTS OTHERS EASILY? WHY OR WHY NOT?

DO YOU BELIEVE PEOPLE ARE TRUSTWORTHY? DO YOU SEE YOURSELF AS TRUSTWORTHY? WHY OR WHY NOT?

IN WHAT WAYS WOULD YOU LIKE TO BECOME MORE TRUSTING?

IN WHAT WAYS WOULD YOU LIKE TO BECOME MORE TRUSTWORTHY?

VULNERABILITY HANGOVERS

YOU KNOW THE FEELING: YOU SHARED JUST A BIT TOO MUCH ABOUT YOURSELF last night. Maybe you were drunk, maybe you were just high on the feeling of being heard. Either way, you woke up with a pit in your stomach, trying to remember what you said. That's called a vulnerability hangover. Unlike regular hangovers, vulnerability hangovers can't be slept off. These hangovers are less about your body detoxing from poison and more about growing pains. It just takes some getting used to. The worst thing we can do is let a vulnerability hangover convince us that we should never open up again.

When we're first learning to be vulnerable with others, we can expect to feel this sense of overexposure often. Learning how much to share and with whom is a process of trial and error. There's no way to do it perfectly. I REPEAT: there is no way to do it perfectly. You will overdo and underdo it when it comes to self-disclosure. The key is to be prepared, and to be very, very nice to yourself. Here are some other tips for managing a vulnerability hangover:

Rest. Give yourself a break. Growing pains of any kind take a lot out of us. When we've opened up more than we're used to, we may have a natural, healthy desire to pull in for a couple days. If you're feeling this, trust it. Take a nap. Go for an easy walk. Have a low-stimulation day.

Reach Out. Contact the person you think you shared too much with. Ask how they felt about the conversation. Let them know you're feeling embarrassed. If it feels right, ask for reassurance. You may find that they're feeling the same way, or that they may have greatly appreciated your openness. If they're an asshole about it, then you know that they're an asshole. That's on them, not you. Maybe they're not a safe person to open up to.

Practice Compassion. When we're feeling embarrassed, it's important to give ourselves massive doses of empathy. Shame is never helpful, so remember that you are far from the only person who's felt this. Everyone has secrets they'd be scared to share. Give yourself credit for being brave and remember that you're never alone in this feeling.

In addition to the difficult feelings associated with a night of oversharing, be prepared for:

New Insights About Old Events. After moments of big expression or big connection, we may find ourselves having new insights about old aspects of our life. We may start to see our careers or relationships in a new light, which can be surprising and overwhelming. Try journaling or talking with someone about the thoughts you're having. Let your feelings ebb and flow, and give yourself time to process what's coming up.

New Frustrations About Existing Relationships. With new insights can come new frustrations. New relationships can offer new perspectives. Once we start to develop relationships with people with whom we can really open up, we may start to become aware of the ways we don't feel comfortable opening up in other relationships. This is to be expected. Personal growth always impacts our relationships, so don't panic. Let new feelings evolve, and be patient with yourself.

START AT THE BEGINNING

THERE'S AN ART TO HOSTING A MEETING. WHETHER IT'S A FAMILY MEETING, BOOK CLUB, or group therapy, there are certain features that make a group atmosphere feel safe, stable, and fun. Throughout the remainder of this book, I'll offer instructions for group activities that will require a basic awareness of how to host an event. Don't be scared! Hosting can be fairly easy if you stick to these principles. No need to memorize them now. As you move through the activities, feel free to refer back to these pages for a refresher on the basics. Just have a look now to familiarize yourself with the concepts.

VENUE MENU

After deciding to start a group, you have to figure out where to host it. Some groups are best hosted in homes. In this case, you can either choose one person's home to host indefinitely or, my preference, switch it up. If you decide to switch it up, make a calendar. Do not decide week by week. If someone commits to hosting and cancels within the week more than once, they should be temporarily barred from hosting until they can ensure that they won't need to cancel again.

Sometimes, groups require spaces that aren't personal homes, or no homes are available for hosting. In these cases, I have found the following types of venues to be great options:

- *Yoga and dance studios*
- *Community centers*
- *High school, college, or other gymnasiums*
- *Private rooms in libraries*
- *Event spaces in apartment buildings*
- *Concert halls during off hours*
- *Private rooms in restaurants and bars*
- *Private outdoor spaces at parks or in people's yards*

If a venue charges a fee, I encourage a pay-what-you-can model to allow all interested folks to attend without forcing the host to front the whole bill. Feel free to let people in the group know what you're being charged. Create a suggested donation amount, like $10 per person. Remind people more than once, and especially at the end, how to pay. Often, folks want to financially support the groups they're a part of if they're able, so give them the chance to!

VIRTUAL GATHERINGS

After COVID, many of our gatherings went online and stayed there. While we may sometimes get sick of sitting in front of computers, virtual gatherings can be a beautiful alternative when health risks or distance keeps us from coming together in person.

Most of the activities in this book can be transferred to digital versions, so long as someone has an account allowing multiple people to join a video chat lasting more than an hour. Just remember to wear pants.

ROLES

Clear roles help groups feel more organized. They also help people feel more invested, and make groups more democratic by allowing multiple members to contribute in a meaningful way. Typically, a group is led by whoever had the idea to start it. Delegating roles gives that person a break, and keeps them from gaining too much power over the group.

Depending on the style of meeting, a variety of roles may be needed. Below is a list of the general roles I believe will be needed for the activities laid out in this book. Feel free to tweak them depending on your particular group format.

Facilitator. This is the person who does the check-in and checkout, who commits to enforcing any rules if necessary (like, say, if people are talking during a nonverbal portion of an event), and who plans the content ahead of time. This person should be comfortable speaking in front of others.

Coordinator. This person will coordinate with the venue or host(s), plan meeting times ahead, and communicate necessary information like directions and schedule to the group. They will be the one to keep track of members' contact information and also be the one who arrives first, unlocks the doors, sets up, and cleans afterward.

Tech Assistant. If any gear is needed for your meetings (like speakers, seating, journals, or refreshments), this person will be the one to acquire it. If you're the tech assistant, make sure to ask group members to pay you back for what you spend! Don't be a hero! Manage your own resentment!

THE CHECK-IN

Check-ins give your group a chance to arrive together in the space, settle, and get comfortable. In a world as fast-paced as ours, I'm honestly shocked how often people fail to do a check-in. As far as I'm concerned, check-ins should be happening at the beginning of every interaction. If you call me and start rattling off a long story before asking how I'm doing, where I physically am, or contextualizing what type of information you're about to tell me, I'm probably not going to receive it as well.

Check-ins are respectful. They honor that all attendees just came from different environments, and are likely still carrying some of that with them. Before I begin a therapy session, I try to do a quick check-in. If the person just had a fender bender on the way to the session, they'll probably be in a different mood than someone who accidentally got there two hours early and has been waiting in the lobby. Checking in gives people a chance to share how they're showing up. If you do nothing else from this list, a check-in alone will likely be enough to keep a gathering from being a disaster. Here's the anatomy of a group check-in.

Sit in a Circle. Circles are just always better. There are occasions when it makes sense for one person to be at the front of a room talking to everyone else, but I typically try to avoid those occasions. Circles are egalitarian, they create an informal yet structured feeling, and they allow everyone to see everyone else. You can use floor seating, chair seating, or a mix to accommodate the needs of those attending. But start with your circle.

Take a Breath. Before beginning any kind of event, I like to give people a chance to take a moment to settle. We're all normally so hurried and distracted, I feel it's never a bad idea. You can either announce this by suggesting that everyone take one to three deep breaths together, or you can just wait to start talking for thirty to sixty seconds. Rushing in is not the way.

Do Introductions. Before beginning any event, you'll want to give everyone a chance to state their name and pronouns. People probably know how to do this, but if you need to explain, you can just say:

"Hey everybody, welcome. Before we begin, let's go around the circle and state our names, pronouns, and a few words about what we're arriving with."

I learned about the phrase "What are you arriving with?" from an authentic relating group based in Montreal called AR-GO. I love how beautifully it frames the check-in, and how it specifically inquires about the aspects of someone's day they may be carrying with them into the room. Someone could answer by talking about how they feel physically ("I'm arriving with a headache") or a memory ("I'm arriving with stress because I just got into a fender bender on the way here") or a current emotional state ("I'm arriving with anxiety because I haven't been around a group of people in a long time"). This question makes space for all those responses. But also, feel free to ask in your own words how folks are feeling.

You might wonder: Should people share their first name only or first and last? Does everyone have to state their pronouns or just those who want to? How much should people share about how they're feeling?

Great questions that I can't answer. It will depend on the size and sort of group you're hosting. Don't stress about particulars. Just give people the chance to introduce themselves and notice who's there, but don't force anyone to share information they're not comfortable offering.

THE RUNDOWN

Before beginning an activity, it can be helpful to give people the rundown of what to expect. This is a trauma-informed choice, as clarity is necessary for consent to take place. If people know what they're getting themselves into, they are able to consciously choose which activities they want to engage in. This also helps people mentally prepare, which can put them at ease. Here are the points I like to include in my rundown:

Tell Folks the Basic Agenda for the meeting, including starting and ending times. Stick to these!

Give People Permission to Leave if they need to—to use the restroom, get some water, or even go home, if that's what feels right. At AR-GO, they call this "honoring yourself." Give people permission to honor themselves. Let them know how they can leave, as well as where they might go if they need to take a call or have a moment alone.

Ask People to Honor One Another. Remind them that the group is a place of mutual respect, and that if anyone behaves in a way that threatens another's sense of safety or agency, they may be asked to leave. Be prepared to ask someone to leave. (It's rarely necessary, but it does happen.)

TURN STYLES

When sharing in a group, there are a couple different ways to negotiate turn-taking.

Popcorn Style, where the group meeting opens and whoever wants to share can take a turn as they wish.

Circular Sharing, where you start with one person in the group and go around, giving people the option to pass if they don't want to share at that time. When using this option, you can make a full circle and then ask if those who didn't choose to share the first time would like to speak then, or, if there's time, if anyone would like to share again.

Choose one style and stick with it for each group.

THE CHECKOUT

Checkouts follow basically the same process as check-ins, except that you don't really need to share introductions again. Checkouts give everyone a chance to feel a sense of unity before closing, and can allow folks to express gratitude for one another and the meeting. In closing, I typically say:

"Thanks again for coming. Before we close, let's go around the circle one more time. If you'd like to, you're welcome to share a couple of words about how you're feeling now. Feel free to pass."

One of the trickiest things about hosting is knowing how to gracefully cut someone off if they're talking too long, which absolutely will happen. I cannot tell you how many times I've seen one person hold a whole group hostage by talking for five or more minutes about how the group has changed their life which, while beautiful and sweet, can keep others from having a chance to share or make them feel guilty if they actually need to leave.

As host, it's your responsibility to find a way to let people know they need to keep shares brief or to cut them off if they forget this. I like to do this with nonverbals at first, by trying to get the attention of the person speaking and gently touching my watch (or the place where one would be) to let them know to wrap it up. If this doesn't work, I say something like:

"Oops, sorry to cut you off, but we need to make sure everyone has a chance to speak. Thanks for sharing."

ALL DRESSED UP AND NOWHERE TO GO

IN HIGH SCHOOL, MY BEST FRIEND, EMILY, AND I WERE those girls who hung out at parties with thirtysomethings when we were sixteen. Yikes. As much fun as we had drinking beer in weird apartments that I, as a thirtysomething, would be too scared to enter now, most of our best times were spent at home, getting ready to go out. We often spent hours trying on clothes, and fixing and refixing our hair, while we talked about dreams and crushes and fights with our families. We'd say we were about to leave, then our favorite sad song would come on, and suddenly we'd be crying our mascara off and falling asleep on top of her bed, our party clothes still on.

Even though I didn't realize it at the time, my understanding of what intimacy can be was informed in large part by these nights with Emily. We rarely think to do things like this on purpose, but sometimes a cry session with friends is just what the doctor ordered. Call me weird, but I'd say it beats most parties. Here's how to plan a going-nowhere gathering.

WHO

Any of your friends who can get down with some bummer vibes. As many people as you want—just don't invite anyone who will make fun of you for crying!!

WHEN

Weekend evenings feel the most fun to me for this kind of event. Since there's often pressure to go out and do something wild on the weekend, staying in and crying with your friends on a Friday feels extra rebellious. But really, any evening will work.

WHERE

Whoever has the comfiest couch is hosting, and they should plan for some people to stay the night.

WHAT

You'll need a fun or fancy outfit, mascara that isn't waterproof, and lots (and lots) of snacks. You may want to create a list of sad movies and songs beforehand. If so, start a group chat and send a collaborative list out so everyone can add to it.

HOW

Plan to get ready together. Bring your makeup bag, your hair supplies, whatever. If you drink, make some cocktails together and play your tunes.

Ask each other questions, like:

- *What's the most difficult thing you've survived this year?*
- *What sadness do you carry that you thought would be gone by now?*
- *What's your favorite sad song/movie/book? What scene affects you most and why?*
- *What do you wish people noticed about you more often?*
- *What do you think people get wrong about you?*
- *What's one thing you wish you had done differently?*

Once you're all dolled up and dishing about your deepest, darkest secrets, take a group selfie. Bonus points if you're lying in a cuddle puddle on the floor and/or someone's mascara is running everywhere. Hang it in a big frame in your hallway like a classic family photo.

CUDDLE PUDDLE

AS A CHILD, WHENEVER I'D STAY OVER WITH friends, I'd get in trouble for spooning them in my sleep. Well, sort of spooning, sort of smothering. I prefer to call it cuddling. I blame my grandma, who let me sleep quite literally on top of her for [redacted] years. I'm not even sure how that was comfortable for either of us, but it must have been because it became so second nature that at sleepovers I'd just crawl right on top of my unsuspecting friends and slobber on them, while totally asleep.

Cuddle puddles are a bit like this, but even better, because everyone involved is awake (at least at the beginning). If you're not familiar with them, "cuddle puddles" are exactly what they sound like: a bunch of people in a big pile, cuddling together. If you've ever been to a really good party, you may have seen one. Or maybe you've seen a basket of kittens curled up together, doing that making-biscuits thing.

The concept isn't new. Humans have been cuddling forever. It's in our blood. But our tech-centered world has changed the nature of touch. With the amount of time most of us spend talking to people through little screens, even non-touchy people are in need of cuddles. *Skin hunger* is a term for the physical and emotional effects of a lack of healthy touch. Studies have shown that skin hunger can cause mental and emotional distress, and can also exacerbate preexisting conditions such as anxiety, loneliness, and depression.

Touch does a lot of great things for our minds and bodies quickly. Touch stimulates pressure sensors under the skin that send messages to the vagus nerve (a very important part of your nervous system related to emotional regulation), causing your heart rate to slow and blood pressure to decrease. This lowers levels of stress hormones such as cortisol, and increases serotonin levels. It boosts immune function, helping protect us from illness and heal from a variety of conditions including HIV and cancer. Touch can help cure insomnia and create more restful sleep cycles. It significantly reduces sensitivity to pain and relieves anxiety in the presence of threat (an effect even more acutely felt when the touch comes from someone we love).

When we cuddle, our brains produce a chemical called oxytocin, known affectionately as the "love drug." Oxytocin produces a feeling of relaxation, warmth, and affection for those around you. In short, oxytocin makes you feel good. Critical in the process of childbirth and breastfeeding, oxytocin facilitates bonding between people and intensifies social memory, causing us to remember people and feel bonded to them for longer. But be careful, oxytocin has been shown to reinforce both pleasant and unpleasant memories. So if you want to remember a conversation or a feeling for a long time, have it while cuddling. And if you can sense that you're having a conversation you'll want to forget, avoid cuddling at all costs.

Interestingly, oxytocin also makes us more likely to exclude or even betray others, but only if it's to defend a person or group we've bonded with. Think of this as the Bonnie and Clyde effect.

What this shows is that touch is a primary means of bonding, and a powerful one. The people we develop a touch-based relationship with have a higher chance of becoming close attachments we're willing to take risks to protect. So if your skin is hungry or you're ready to form some ride-or-die connections, here's your guide to hosting a cuddle puddle!

WHO

The key to hosting a top-notch cuddle puddle is the right guest list. Unlike other events, I recommend being somewhat exclusive about who you invite to a cuddle puddle. Only those who know how to set and honor boundaries should be there. Look for people who have demonstrated an ability and willingness to hear and respect no. Anyone who has pressured someone to date them, have sex with them, or even hang out with them should not be invited, unless they've done a lot of work to change those habits. Cuddle puddles vary in size and form, but they are typically platonic. One of the most important benefits of such an event is the ability to receive nonsexual touch. Nothing against sexual touch (big fan), but for those of us who grew up in cultures where touch is thought of as something only lovers do, it can be extremely healing to know we can get this good medicine from friends, or even strangers. Yep, touch can happen between people who just met. If the situation is set up well, cuddle puddles can be practiced with friends, lovers, family, or any group of people, as long as all participants respect one another.

WHERE

One key to hosting a great cuddle event is ensuring that you have a comfy place to host it. I've done cuddle puddles outside and they're fine, but bugs usually infringe on my fullest enjoyment. Living room floors are a favorite space for group cuddles, but large enough beds will do as well. As always, we want the space to be clean, safe, and smell good (or at least not bad). If your puddle will be on the floor, I recommend putting down yoga mats, a mattress pad, or a few blankets stacked on top of one another. You'll also want to wear comfy clothes so nobody gets stuck with a belt buckle in their back. And try to avoid perfumes or any strong scents.

ABSOLUTELY NO PHONES IN THE CUDDLE PUDDLE!!!

HOW

Before beginning, everyone should understand the rules. Make sure to state these explicitly while you have everyone's attention, and make sure they all agree. These include:

- *No touching anywhere that underwear goes*
- *Always do a verbal check-in before spooning or massaging*
- *No questions asked if someone says no*

Again, cuddle puddles are not about hooking up. If you find yourself thinking about that, no shame. Just gently remind yourself that this is not the time for that, and excuse yourself, if necessary. Cuddle puddles are about remembering that we're animals in little bodies crawling around on the earth together. They're about holding each other's hands and faces until there are no thoughts left about it, until we're not wondering whether it's weird or if they want to let go or if their hand is falling asleep. They're about holding each other while we think our own thoughts—as if we're alone, as if their body is just an extension of ours, which it is.

Either before or after an event, it can be useful to reflect on your feelings about touch. Notice what works for you and what doesn't. Don't be afraid to get specific about your preferences and learn as you go!

WHAT IS YOUR RELATIONSHIP WITH TOUCH? ARE YOU MORE COMFORTABLE WITH CERTAIN KINDS OF TOUCH OR TOUCH FROM CERTAIN KINDS OF PEOPLE?

WHAT BARRIERS DO YOU FEEL TOWARD TOUCH THAT YOU'D LIKE TO LET GO OF?

WAS TOUCH COMMON IN YOUR HOUSEHOLD GROWING UP? WHAT KIND? HOW DID YOU FEEL ABOUT IT?

IF YOU WERE ABLE TO FEEL NO ANXIETY ABOUT PHYSICAL CONTACT, HOW WOULD YOU LIKE TO BE TOUCHED? WHERE? BY WHOM? HOW WOULD YOU LIKE TO TOUCH OTHERS?

PARTY POSITIONS

PITY PARTY FAVORS

TISSUES

BLANKETS

NOTEPADS AND PENS

TEA AND WATER

FUZZY SLIPPERS

SNACKS

TOWN CRIER CHOIR

I sing and sing of awful things, the pleasure
that my sadness brings.

—Bright Eyes

OMAHA, NEBRASKA, ISN'T EXACTLY KNOWN FOR BEING AN EMOTIONALLY OPEN PLACE.
The affirming messages I received as a child were largely at odds with the culture
around me, which emphasized politeness and decorum above frankness and authentic-
ity. What Omaha is known for is its music scene. Lucky for me, that hit its peak in the
early 2000s, when I was in high school. Back then, Saddle Creek Records was turning
out a whole lineup of nationally acclaimed bands making sad emo, which my friends
and I were basically obsessed with. Most weekends, we put on black eyeliner and skinny
jeans and cry-sang along with their depressing anthems at packed local shows. As I got
a bit older and started dating in this scene, I mistakenly assumed that anyone who loves
or makes sad music would be comfortable talking about sadness. False. I've made many
a midwestern party weird by trying to talk about feelings, which taught me several
things, including: (a) I shouldn't date musicians, and (b) singing about sadness is easier
for most people than talking about it.

Singing, especially in a community setting, is a time-honored tradition. It's been
shown to promote a sense of social inclusion. Some anthropologists believe that singing

in groups played an important role in ancient social bonding. Singing with others creates feelings of closeness and belonging relatively quickly, and in circumstances where one-to-one bonding is not possible. In the modern era, as social division and loneliness have become rampant, social singing offers an easy, cheap solution.

Singing also has physiological benefits, such as boosting production of antibodies that strengthen immune response, and triggering the release of endorphins, resulting in higher pain tolerance. Singing also improves oxygen levels and enhances memory function. Singing with others helps us process grief and even establish meaning and group solidarity during times of war.

Despite my bad luck at parties, I was fortunate enough to meet many like-minded friends during my time in Omaha, people who wanted to sing *and* talk about feelings. In my early twenties I joined Aetherplough, a performance troupe that (among other things) sang together every winter. During the coldest months of the year, we'd gather around fireplaces and curate a list of favorite folk and pop songs to arrange as choral pieces. We drank whiskey and hot cocoa as we practiced, before eventually performing them downtown for passersby. No one was ever asked to audition, and you didn't have to be able to hit any special notes to join. The point was catharsis, not perfect pitch. I know I'm not the only person who found great healing in this experience, and many of us formed relationships through singing together that have now lasted decades. Here's a guide to forming a choir of your own.

In the dark times, will there also be singing?
Yes, there will also be singing. About the dark times.

—Bertolt Brecht

WHO

Anyone who wants to sing can join. As far as I'm concerned, the more, the merrier. There are benefits to both a commitment-based system, which discourages people from missing meetings, and a come-as-you-can system, where folks can join at any time. Choose which style makes sense for you and your crew.

WHEN

I find that Sunday afternoon or evening works well, as people often have the time off and aren't out partying. You'll need at least three hours for practice, depending on group size. Weekly meetings are best, whether you're building toward a performance or not. Any more time between meetings and you might forget your parts!

WHERE

In my experience, living rooms make great rehearsal spaces. Depending on the weather in your area, you could meet in the park. Since choir practice sounds very wholesome and normal, you may also be able to get a local church or community center to offer the use of a room for free.

HOW

As with any group meeting, establishing roles is a good idea. Even if the tasks are simple, clarifying ahead of time who will do what can be extremely helpful. Here are a couple jobs you'll want to fill:

Choir Coordinator. This person will establish meeting times and locations, gather contact information, and communicate necessary information to the group. If you're rehearsing at a community center, the coordinator will make calls on behalf of the group and serve as the point of contact. They may also take on the job of supplying essential items like tissues or drinks.

Music Director. This person will help establish the song list (ideally by taking group suggestions and/or voting), print out lyrics before meetings, and help people determine their parts. Depending on the preferences of the group, you can establish parts by soprano, alto, tenor, bass classifications, or you can just make it up as you go.

Part Leads. In my choir days, there was usually someone in charge of each vocal part. The soprano lead, for example, would help choose the high vocal part for each song and assist others in learning it.

Instrumental Accompanist(s). You may also want someone to provide accompaniment by playing guitar or piano. They don't have to be pro, as simple chord progressions should suffice. It can also be helpful to have someone holding the tempo with a drum or tambourine. If you don't plan to have accompaniment, you can use a backing track. Karaoke versions of many songs are available for free online, but if you can't find those, just use the original track and sing along with the artist.

Tech Assistant. If you're using speakers, microphones, or instruments as part of your accompaniment, you'll want someone to be in charge of locating and maintaining these. If not, you won't need this person.

One of the best parts of the process is choosing your songs. In a 2008 interview with NPR, musician Brian Eno talked about his experience with small group choirs, and discussed how to choose songs that work well for a variety of singers. He suggested blues, rock, and country songs as they typically feature basic chord structures and are easier to learn. He also encouraged groups to choose songs that are "word-rich" and "vowel-rich," as they make it easier for singers to stay in time with one another.

Practice should be fun! Always leave an hour for mingling at the end, as people will be socially lubricated and likely eager to chat. Public performance is optional, and you'll experience many of the same benefits without choosing to showcase your talent for others. But if you do decide to perform, try to pick a time, location, and set list at least two months in advance. This way, everyone can give friends and family notice, and you'll have plenty of time to practice.

When it comes time to perform, I encourage dressing up. Consider choosing a group theme for your attire, like the color red or outfits inspired by a certain era. Bring your own flasks and folders for music. Invite your friends and family and coworkers and random people on the street.

DANCING WITH MYSELVES

HAVE YOU EVER THOUGHT ABOUT WHAT YOU WOULD DO IF YOU FOUND OUT THE WORLD was ending tomorrow? I have, and you know what my answer is? Dance. At almost every awful moment in my life, I've danced. Not danced like tap-dancing, or doing pirouettes (don't know how), or dancing to look sexy. Not even close. I'm talking about sacred dancing. Dancing as prayer, the kind of dancing that sometimes looks like crawling on the floor in silence.

Humans have long turned to dance in times of hardship. As far as we know, dancing became a widespread social practice around 3000 BC in Egypt, when dancing became a central feature of religious rites and ceremonies. Only relatively recently have people in the West started thinking of dance as an activity reserved for lighthearted fun. We do ourselves a great disservice when we see dance as something only some people can do, or something we need to train to do, or something we need an excuse or good music to do. None of these things are true. Dance is actually for everyone, regardless of body type or ability. It's for moments of joy and pain. If you've ever attended an ecstatic dance event, you've probably seen this Rumi quote on a tapestry:

Dance, when you're broken open. Dance, if
you've torn the bandage off. Dance in the
middle of the fighting. Dance in your blood.
Dance when you're perfectly free.

—Rumi

Rumi was a Sufi mystic, so he understood the power of dance. Sufis practice a form of movement meditation called whirling, wherein participants listen to music and spin in circles until they attain a trancelike state in which they can more easily experience their connection with the divine. This kind of dance isn't about doing any impressive moves, it's about losing yourself. It's about touching the rapture of being alive, and quieting the part of us that wants to control everything.

For years, I helped run an ecstatic dance group with friends. Ecstatic dance is a free-form movement meditation used by people across faiths to attain a state of heightened awareness and ecstasy. Many people also misunderstand the word "ecstasy." It isn't about feeling totally high on good vibes, it's about a feeling of transcending oneself, and feeling more in tune with all of life around you. Ecstatic dance resembles many ancient forms of ritual dance, and can be incorporated into grief rituals or celebrations. During the time I helped run that group, my fellow dancers and I met almost every Sunday morning as a sort of alternative church. In zero ways did our events resemble clubbing or performance. People in mourning came to dance with us. People diagnosed with terminal illnesses came to dance with us. Almost every one of us cried at some point during our dances. No one asked why we were crying or tried to fix it, they just let us cry. Everyone understood.

When I dance, I find that many divergent parts of me—the social parts and the solitary parts, the sad parts and the happy parts—can be reunited. After a good dance session, I feel more like myself. I also feel less concerned about how others are perceiving me but somehow also more available for connection. I know it will be a tough sell for some folks, but dancing provides an amazing opportunity to connect with yourself and others in an embodied and emotionally liberating way. But don't just take my word for it: in addition to its obvious impact on physical health, researchers have found that dancing stimulates our brain's reward centers, increases confidence, help us set and achieve goals, reduces the risk of dementia, and functions as an effective coping skill for those who are actively surviving traumatic circumstances. Here's a simple guide for starting your own dance group!

WHO

People of all backgrounds and body types can join this practice. No dance experience is required. Groups of any size should be fine, depending on location. Very small children may have a hard time with the nonverbal portion (there should be no speaking while dancing), so you may want to set an age limit.

WHEN

I've heard of ecstatic dance groups taking place on any day, morning or night. I loved our Sunday morning time slot because most people arrived sleepy and sober. Different times provide different benefits. We usually planned for three hours from start to fin-ish: an hour to set up and open, an hour of dancing, and an hour to mingle and clean.

WHERE

This activity requires quite a bit of space. Yoga and dance studios are ideal, but gyms and community centers could work, too. You'll want to choose a place with a cleanish floor and, depending on climate, air-conditioning and heat. Natural or low lighting is ideal, as is privacy. Mirrors are a bonus!

NO PHONES ON THE DANCE FLOOR!! I MEAN IT!

HOW

Hippies don't like rules, but they're necessary. If you're going to run a healing group of any kind, structure helps to ensure that the space feels predictable and safe. Without rules, events can feel chaotic and anxiety-producing. Protecting the energy of a space is a part of the responsibility of anyone who chooses to lead an event. We can't ever be sure that others are showing up in a nonjudgmental state of mind, but we can make sure to speak with them if their behavior feels unsafe or mean-spirited.

While the practice itself is relatively simple and open-ended, there can be a bit of prep work to do. Our group assigned people these roles to help keep things simple:

DJ. Each time you meet, someone will need to provide the music. My suggestion is to prepare an hour-long playlist before and play it through a Bluetooth speaker system. Almost any genre can work. I was trained to create playlists that begin slowly, build to a faster pace, and then drop back down again. I've seen folks use live DJs or musicians for ecstatic dance events also. I prefer the more contemplative feeling of a closed group and prerecorded music, but I know others love the live DJ vibe as well.

Venue Coordinator. Someone should be the point person at the venue. This person can also arrive early, unlock doors, set up an altar space, if you choose to have one, turn the lights down, and clean up afterward. They should be the one who communicates with the group about location, timing, and directions.

Facilitator. Pick a person who will open and close the group meetings. Again, this person should be comfortable speaking in front of others, as whoever initiates the circle will set the energetic tone for the hour. Feel free to wing it or use the script offered below.

Optional Check-in Script:

Hello and welcome! We're here to move together through the practice of ecstatic dance. Ecstatic dance is a free-form movement meditation practiced in a nonjudgmental space. It's an opportunity to come back into our bodies and get in touch with what emotion and energy we may be holding on to that wants to move through us.

This is an unguided practice, meaning that as long as we are respecting ourselves and one another, there's no wrong way to do it. Ecstatic dance is not performative. While we may witness one another as we interact in the space, the purpose of our dance is not to look cool or impressive but to come back into conversation with our bodies.

Once we begin, this is a nonverbal space. We are free to sing or make sounds, but we do not have conversations using words. If you need to have a conversation, please step outside. This includes text conversations. Please keep cell phones silent and tucked away by the door.

Before we begin, let's go around the circle and share our names. If you'd like to state a brief intention for your dance (such as "let go of stress," or "try something new"), feel free to share that now. Feel free to pass.

People introduce themselves

If the person who created the playlist would like to say anything about the mood or intention of the music, do that now.

Now, everyone, please find your own space around the room. Let's dance!

Optional Checkout Script:

Once the music stops, the facilitator will take a moment and then begin to speak again:

When you're ready, please come back together for our closing circle.

In closing, we'll go around the circle again. If you'd like to, share one to three words that reflect how you're feeling now.

People say words

Thank you for coming.

I like to end by having everyone put their hands on the floor and drumming together. People usually begin drumming slowly and naturally build to a faster rhythm. At some point, people start slapping the ground really hard and laughing. It's a good time.

NO UTOPIA

GIVING UP ON
A PERFECT WORLD

ALL VIBES MATTER

> After every atrocity one can expect to hear the
> same predictable apologies: it never happened;
> the victim lies; the victim exaggerates; the
> victim brought it upon herself; and in any case
> it is time to forget the past and move on.
>
> —Judith Lewis Herman

AS MUCH AS I WANT PEOPLE TO TALK OPENLY ABOUT THEIR PAIN, IT WOULD BE NAIVE OF me to overlook how much identity impacts the way that expression is received. Whether our suffering is met with empathy or suspicion has everything to do with who we are. Factors like race, gender, class, disability status, sexual orientation, and more deeply impact the way others perceive us, and our expressions of pain are no exception. Pain is inherently political. Whose pain we talk about is political. Whose pain we ignore is political. Whose pain we believe is real and worthy of a response is political. Politics isn't some abstract debate about ideas, it's how we treat the people we don't know. As a white woman, I can generally trust that my tears will be met with concern, or at least not be seen as a threat to others. The same is not true for BIPOC people, or people of other marginalized identities who may be met with disbelief, criticism, even contempt when they openly share their suffering.

This skepticism applies to both emotional and physical pain. Research has shown that Black patients in the United States are routinely doubted when describing their symptoms to medical professionals, and are given less pain medication for the same ailments as their white peers. Many medical students even believe racist myths, like that Black people experience less pain because they have thicker skin, which likely ties back to dangerous, now-debunked claims made by physicians in the 1800s. This historic mistreatment of BIPOC individuals perpetuates health disparities in the United States, as people of color who have come to expect disrespect may be more likely to put off seeking medical treatment until symptoms are severe.

Over the last several years, we've also witnessed the rise of the #MeToo movement, which was initiated in 2006 by activist Tarana Burke as a way to encourage survivors of sexual assault to share their experiences and seek support in one another. While much social healing has occurred as a result, the initiative has also shed light on the skepticism many feel toward women and survivors. Those who speak out are regularly accused of manipulation and slander, and often experience threats or actual acts of violence toward them as a result. To add insult to injury, any inconsistency in a survivor's testimony is likely to be brutally scrutinized and framed as proof that they are either lying or mentally unstable. In reality, difficulty remembering exact details of any event is extremely common, and those who have experienced acute trauma know that memories of psychologically overwhelming events are often even more fragmented.

Society's tendency to doubt survivors not only keeps many people from reporting an assault, but also opens them up to significant additional trauma. Male survivors of assault experience a unique tension when it comes to this issue. While men are less likely to be assaulted, they are also less likely to report. Traditional perceptions of masculinity perpetuate the misconception that men always want sex, which can lead to automatic dismissal of any man's claims of sexual abuse. When they do report the event, they often experience shaming from other men who see assault as an affront to a man's dominance.

We know that homophobia places LGBTQ individuals at an increased risk of suicide and issues like anxiety and depression, but less is known about the impact of doubt on the mental health of queer folks. Coming out can be a traumatic experience, especially if the response one receives is of disbelief. Statements like "You'll grow out of it" and "You can't be sure of that" are not only dismissive, they discourage the person coming out from discussing that aspect of their life again. Internalized homophobia, which includes not only negative feelings about one's queer identity but also distrust that queer desire is even valid or real, is also a major concern, as it's been linked to health issues and poorer overall quality of life.

As anyone with an invisible illness or disability will tell you, skepticism is a routine occurrence. Living with a chronic health condition is hard enough. Being expected to constantly prove that your symptoms are real, or being repeatedly asked to justify why you need accommodations, can be downright dehumanizing (not to mention exhausting). Likewise, those with severe mental illness are often met with messages of diminishment which others may even think are supportive. "Just get out of bed, that'll make you feel better" or "Maybe you just need some fresh air" are common responses to hearing that someone's depression is impacting their functioning. While certain behaviors and lifestyle modifications may genuinely help relieve symptoms, implying that feeling better is simple or easily accomplished reveals a misunderstanding of the seriousness of what these individuals are going through.

When you're constantly met with disbelief, it can be easy to absorb these messages and turn them against yourself. Consistently being told that your pain is not real or that you are exaggerating can cause some to question whether their suffering is actually imaginary or "not that bad." Moira is a first-generation, mixed-race woman in her twenties who spent years trying to make sense of her chronic pain and fatigue. In our conversations about her health, she often oscillated between doubting that she could possibly feel as bad as she does and becoming angry that her mostly white, male doctors would not take her seriously. When she did finally receive a diagnosis that explained the pain she'd been in for years, she felt both relieved and saddened that she'd been made to question her own intuition. After a lifetime of conditioning, it can take years to recover a sense of trust that we even know what we're feeling.

EMPATHY AND PRIVILEGE

> When you're accustomed to privilege,
> equality feels like oppression.
>
> **—Anonymous activist adage**

If it's bad enough to feel like your pain isn't trusted, it's worse to feel like people believe you but just don't care. Empathy and privilege go hand in hand. In fact, the entire conversation about privilege could be reframed as a conversation about pain. To be privileged is to trust that your pain will be met with belief, empathy, and assistance. Not only do we tend to dismiss the accounts of marginalized people, we also tend to deem their pain less worthy of concern. Not enough is said about the incredible amount of courage it takes to trust oneself and express one's hurt in a world that consistently tells you not to. To assert that your pain is valid when doing so means risking accusations and threats to your safety is nothing short of heroic. The fact that so many people are faced with this dilemma speaks volumes about the culture we've collectively built, where empathy is seen as a scarce resource reserved for the most elite. Everyone, regardless of identity, deserves empathy, but the reality is that many don't get it.

Not all failure to empathize is the result of prejudice, of course. Sometimes we simply miss other people's cues. We're all bound by the limitations of our life experience; it's easier to empathize with people whose experience we can relate to. Research has also shown that people with high levels of social privilege tend to be less empathetic while lower socioeconomic status has been linked with more accurate assessment of the feelings of others. The solution isn't that those who are more privileged should rush out and try to experience trauma. Instead, we should all simply commit to becoming more empathetic. The problem lies not in our struggle to understand each other's pain but in our belief that we don't have to try. Feeling entitled to ignorance is worse than the ignorance itself, which we can always outgrow.

THE FALSE CARE SHORTAGE

One of the ways we justify a position of apathy is through faultfinding. Usually, we do this in our own minds while watching the news: "Why doesn't she just leave him?," or "If you can't afford one kid, why would you have another?" But sometimes we play this thinking out with others through subtle commentary and questioning, like asking sick people, "How much kale do you eat?," or asking survivors, "Why were you wearing that?" In trying to establish whose fault suffering is, we're trying to determine whether we have to care. If somebody "did it to themselves" we feel entitled not to think about their pain. In erecting a wall between us and them, we feel a false sense of control and project an illusion of order onto the world. We tell ourselves that if we make good choices, we won't ever have to experience that kind of pain. This gives us a respite from the anxiety that accompanies a recognition of how often bad things happen to good people.

Sure, sometimes what happens to us is our fault. But that actually doesn't mean we don't deserve care. Part of why we even feel the need to argue about who deserves support is because we think of care as a scarce resource we have to compete with others to deserve. If someone else's pain is worse than ours, we worry that this means they'll move ahead of us in the line and the care will run out before it's our turn. This is why we see people competing in the Trauma Olympics online, fighting to be seen as

"most damaged." That's not a competition anyone actually wants to win. The only rea-son we're willing to degrade ourselves in this way is because we think we have to do so to prove that we're worthy of care. While it may be important to take stock of whose needs are most urgent in some circumstances, there's no reason to believe we can help only those who are in most dire need.

What if, instead of seeing care as something we have to fight one another for, we thought of it as a regenerative resource we each had the power to produce? We may not all be doctors, but we can all offer some type of assistance. Care is not a zero-sum game. It is not a pie that only has a few slices and, if I take one, there's less for you. Care is a garden. When I help you heal, something heals in me. There is no upward limit to what humans can do to help one another, and we don't have to wait for permission from anyone to start offering that help now. Much of what we need to do is simple: listen. Believe people when they tell us they're hurting. Let the pain we witness affect us, and inspire us to show up for each other in the ways we can.

OF THE MANY DEMOGRAPHICS EXPERIENCING DIFFERENT FORMS OF HARDSHIP, WHOSE PAIN DO YOU THINK ABOUT MOST? WHOSE PAIN DO YOU THINK ABOUT LEAST? WHY DO YOU THINK THAT IS?

WHOSE EXPRESSIONS OF PAIN DO YOU FIND MOST EASY TO BELIEVE? WHOSE EXPRESSIONS OF PAIN DO YOU FIND MOST DIFFICULT TO BELIEVE? WHY DO YOU THINK THAT IS?

HAVE YOU EXPERIENCED TIMES WHEN OTHERS DIDN'T SEEM TO BELIEVE OR CARE ABOUT YOUR PAIN? WHAT WAS THAT LIKE FOR YOU?

UNGASLIGHTING GROUP

A FEW YEARS AGO, I WAS HAVING A COCKTAIL AT THE BAR WHERE MY BOYFRIEND worked. One of the regulars, a friend of my now-ex, seemed to have it out for me. He didn't like that I was dating his buddy, so when my ex got busy with other customers and left us alone, he struck up a conversation that immediately devolved into an intense line of questioning. A few inquiries in, he asked me what I do.

"I'm a therapist," I said. He scowled.

"Like, an actual therapist?" he asked, accusingly.

"Um, yes?" I replied, taken off guard. He laughed.

"Okay then, where'd you go to school?"

I answered him, but sheepishly. I was out of my element and started to panic. I looked around for my boyfriend, who was distracted. I took stock of the situation: I was on this dude's turf, he was clearly drunk, and he'd known my boyfriend much longer than I had. I had no real recourse, so I tried to assume the best. "Maybe he's just curious," I thought. "Don't be paranoid," I thought.

He started asking about the sports teams at my graduate school. Mind you, I have never in my life watched a sporting event on purpose, and I had certainly not paid any attention to the athletic calendar while getting my degree. This guy, who was apparently a fan of my school's football team, asked me to prove that I went there by describing the mascot, which I very much failed to do. He seemed to feel satisfied by this, as if he'd rested his case.

"Wow, wooooow," he sang, delighted. "Stop lying. You did not go to school there."

Here's where it gets interesting. At that moment, dear reader, I actually questioned whether he was right. Inside of my expensive, educated brain, I heard this thought: Maybe I am wrong. Did I really go there? What if he's right? Almost immediately, thank God, I was able to walk myself back from that train of thought, and I became visibly furious. I told the guy to fuck off, found my boyfriend, and explained that his friend was accosting me and I was leaving. My now-ex looked genuinely shocked and tried to assure me that couldn't be the case. The next day, as I recounted the conversation in great detail, he continuously tried to cast doubt on the story, to prove that it wasn't that bad.

"Are you sure you weren't just misunderstanding him? He's usually really cool." I could tell that he himself didn't want to believe that his friend had been such a jerk. His questions were as much about convincing himself as me, but they ultimately made it clear that he wasn't willing to believe me. He half-heartedly apologized for his friend's behavior but left our talk shaking his head, sure something had been lost in the wash.

Here's the thing: *gaslighting*, a form of psychological manipulation wherein someone attempts to make another person question their sanity by invalidating their feelings or concerns, is not always a dramatic, overt ruse, though that happens, too—I've worked with several people who have literally had partners or family members try to kill them and then later deny it. The classic example of gaslighting where a man is cheating on a woman and accuses her of being crazy when she suspects it does actually happen. But more often than not, gaslighting is more insidious than that.

Almost everyone has been gaslit, and almost everyone has gaslighted someone else. As in the case with my ex, we often gaslight others because we simply don't want to acknowledge how shitty a situation is. We don't want to accept an ugly truth about someone we love or about the world, so we minimize a person's testimony. We would rather believe they're having a lapse of judgment than that this terrible thing happened. In a way, this is understandable. Believing other people means allowing them to alter our perception of reality, and we don't always want our perception altered. But when we refuse to believe the people in our lives, we leave them alone in their experience. We choose our fantasy over their reality and, in doing so, abandon them.

There's also a cost-benefit analysis happening for the person being gaslit. If the gaslighter seems confident enough, and the thing we're trying to tell them is awful enough, it can be tempting to go with their story. Nobody wants it to be true that their partner pushed them down the stairs or their mother told them they wish they'd never been born. If someone can make us pretend these things didn't happen, we may try to accept that offer. The cost of this option is high, however.

When we override our perception in favor of another person's, we are essentially declaring that we can't trust ourselves. It's one thing to allow another person's take to soften our narrative, but to outright dismiss our experience is to forfeit our internal compass. This puts us in a position of even greater dependency because it means we need someone else to report reality back to us since we don't think we can rely on our senses. If we're gaslit often enough, this switch can be flipped out of exhaustion. It can feel easier to believe we're mentally unstable. We can even start to genuinely feel unstable even if we're not, like we're living inside a novel with an unreliable narrator. The irony is that, in my experience, people who are frequently gaslit often become hyper-logical and very precise in their thinking. Because their emotions have been used as evidence of their lack of credibility, they feel the need to justify any and all feelings of discontent with excessive proof.

When we're being gaslit, we can feel like we're in a fog. Ideas that made sense just moments before suddenly seem murky. The mind goes blank. We feel like Sarah in the Labyrinth after she eats the poisoned peach. We question whether we're remembering things correctly, we start to feel foolish for even bringing something up in the first place. After an episode of gaslighting, we can feel totally defeated. It may take days to recover emotionally, but because we're so embarrassed and likely blaming ourselves for what happened, we can feel scared to talk about it with others. We fear being called crazy. We fear being blamed for having a relationship with a person who gaslights us in the first place. Often, the person doing the gaslighting will try to restore the connection during this time, hoping to bury the event with a mutually agreed upon story, like we were both just tired and needed some rest. So long as we stay stuck in this cycle, we remain too unsure of ourselves to advocate for our well-being.

You might be wondering, What if someone is actually overreacting or being unreasonable? Is telling them that gaslighting? No, it doesn't have to be. Sometimes, a person's fears are unreasonable and they need help being reminded of that. (Revisit Wrong Alarm earlier in the book for a refresher.) If someone is afraid of flying, they want you to tell them that it's unlikely the plane will crash. Much of the difference between gaslighting them and comforting them lies in the delivery.

Gaslighting sounds like, "I don't know what you're talking about. You're so paranoid. It's nothing, you're imagining things."

Comforting sounds like, "I can hear that you're really scared. I'd like to help. Would it be comforting to hear some statistics about how safe flying is?"

Gaslighting can take place in interpersonal relationships as well as on a larger political scale. We see large-scale gaslighting when the harm that a group of people has experienced or is experiencing is minimized, denied, or otherwise invalidated. In the United States, the most obvious example of this social gaslighting is the way many white Americans talk about racism, all but denying it exists or has ever existed. If you've been impacted by gaslighting, know that you absolutely can rebuild trust with yourself. This process involves forgiving yourself for doubting what you knew was true. It involves empathizing with the part of you that may have needed to dismiss your perception to survive. It involves acknowledging that your truth is powerful, that it was threatening enough to others that they felt the need to do this to you. It also involves having your perception validated by other human beings. For that last bit, you can call in the support of others who have been similarly gaslit and start an ungaslighting group!

WHO

An Ungaslighting Group can be formed around any identity factor (race, gender, sexuality) or shared experience (domestic abuse, religious trauma, poverty). The ideal size is between five and twelve people. You want it to be big enough to help you feel that you're not alone but still small enough to give each person a chance to speak. A group of people who already know one another will feel different than a group of people who meet for this purpose, or something in between. Neither is better or worse.

WHEN

An Ungaslighting Group can meet weekly or biweekly for a period of three or six months. I wouldn't advise meeting any less than twice a month to maintain a sense of group coherence, and I wouldn't recommend meeting indefinitely as this can make things feel too casual and less focused over time.

WHERE

Your group can meet in person or online. If you're meeting in person, decide if you'd like to host in one person's home, share hosting duties, or find a local community space. We've already gone over ideas for that option, so I trust y'all can work it out if you go that route.

HOW

When you arrive to your meeting, place chairs in a circle. Make sure all devices are turned off or on silent and that all doors are closed once everyone arrives. Once folks are settled, begin with a check-in. When everyone has had a chance, state the intentions and rules of the group. Here's an optional script for that:

We are gathered here today to ungaslight together. We commit to the work of undoing the damage the world has done in an effort to make us doubt ourselves and each other. In hearing one another's stories, we validate that our perception is trustworthy, and that we are credible interpreters of our own shared reality.

To keep our space safe, we speak only for ourselves and refrain from making comments or judgments about what each person shares. Our job is simply to share what is true for us and to listen and believe what is true for others. While the focus of our group is [identity factor or shared experience], we allow others to share freely about whatever aspect of their life feels relevant and in need of affirmation. We keep our sharing to five minutes each [adjust according to group size] to allow each person a turn.

This group meeting is now open to whoever would like to share.

Using either popcorn style or circular turn-taking, allow each person a chance to speak. When it's your turn, talk about a time/times when your fears, concerns, or desires were dismissed and made to seem unreasonable. Tell the story of an experience, whether recent or from the distant past, when you felt unheard or discounted. Talk about how others treated you and how it made you feel. (Recounting how they treated you is still speaking for yourself!) When you're done, thank the group for listening.

When others are speaking, simply listen. Empathize. Believe them. As tempting as it might be, refrain from making sounds or comments or asking questions. When a person is done, your group is free to come up with some way of acknowledging their share, like finger snaps, or "Thank you," or a simple "We believe you."

That's it. Rinse and repeat, believers. Remember, ungaslighting groups aren't about becoming immune to gaslighting forever. They aren't about believing our perception is always 100 percent accurate. They're simply about finding a way out of the fog, and learning to trust ourselves and each other again.

BATHROOM VOWS

DESPITE EVERYTHING I'VE SAID ABOUT HOW YOU'RE NEVER REALLY ALONE AND HOW, with a bit of intention, you can build a life of connection, you will unfortunately still encounter moments when you feel totally deserted, utterly abandoned by all that's right in the world, and rejected by those who you love. Sorry! If your life is anything like mine, these moments won't arise when you're prepared for them or have access to your altar space or support network. Oh no, they'll come when you're least expecting it. Say, when you're at a "casual" dinner party to which you wore leggings, only to find that your ex is there with his gorgeous new partner who's wearing a literal gown.

No matter how tethered we are to the web of life, we will experience moments when we feel unaccompanied, when we have to lean on ourselves alone. In life there will be times when we'd rather be anywhere but in our own heads. Sadly, no one else can really join us in the black box of our consciousness. This means that we have to try to be good company inside our noggins. We have to find a way to stay with our feelings when we'd much rather not. We have to give a shit about ourselves when it seems like no one else does. In moments like these, when we can't stop to do a full-on ritual or even get much privacy, we still have to commit to ourselves. We have to excuse ourselves, find the nearest bathroom, look at ourselves in the dirty mirror, and say: "You. I still choose you."

Here are your bathroom vows for those moments.

I WILL NOT ABANDON YOU.

I COULDN'T IF I WANTED TO.

PITY OR PARTY, I'M HERE TO STAY

AND I'D HAVE IT NO OTHER WAY.

OF ALL THE PEOPLE WE COULD BE,

I'M GLAD I'M YOU AND YOU ARE ME.

AND DON'T FORGET, OUR ENEMIES

WILL GET WHAT THEY HAVE COMING.

KILL YOUR IDOLS

A pedestal is as much a prison as any small, confined space.

—Gloria Steinem

WHEN I WAS YOUNGER, I REMEMBER THINKING MY AUNT RAYNEE HAD EVERYTHING FIG-ured out. The only one of my grandma's kids who wasn't addicted to drugs, she was the automatic success story. But it wasn't her sobriety alone that made her seem so put together. Raynee always had her hair and nails done. She graduated from college at the conventionally appropriate age and immediately got a stable job in finance. She married a (seemingly) normal man from a supportive family and had two healthy kids by thirty. Yesterday, Raynee and I sat on the phone for three hours, laughing as we took turns asking each other the same, desperate questions about our similarly chaotic lives.

"You were supposed to be the one who told me what to do!" I joked.

"I'm sorry, Chels." She sighed, meaning it. Over the past several years, I'd watched as she had walked away from everything I thought made her life so perfect: her marriage, her longtime job, her performance as "best mother."

"If it helps, I'm happier now." I knew that she meant that too.

We all have role models. People who seem to have gotten a memo we missed.

They're the ones whose papers we cheat off, the ones we turn to when we forget our lines in the drama of life. And while they may be more prepared in some ways, I can assure you they don't know everything.

At first, this realization is a relief. Many of my clients feel incredible peace when they finally accept that their parents are just people who, like them, have been winging it the whole time. This perspective helps us forgive ourselves for failing to achieve the imaginary standard we realize no one else is living up to either. It also helps us forgive those we've placed on a pedestal as we discover that they, too, are just doing their best. Soon, though, this fact becomes scary. If no one knows what's going on, who will lead us through our darkest hour?

Around the time that I was studying to become a therapist, I was heavily involved in Buddhist practice. Having never joined an organized religion before, I'd been shocked to find that so many of the lessons of Buddhism resonate with my sensitive, rebellious heart. One teacher in particular, a Canadian Zen practitioner named Michael Stone, really spoke my language. Trained as a psychotherapist himself, Michael wrote books and delivered lectures to monastic students and laypeople alike. He was young, and his perspective was fresh, incorporating song lyrics and modern art into his talks on ancient Buddhist texts. While I had limited personal interaction with him, his work became a guidepost in my life. I turned to his podcasts and books for help with relational struggles, questions about mortality, even business insight.

In July 2017, news broke that Michael was in a coma. Two days later, he died in a hospital in British Columbia, surrounded by friends and family. His death felt sudden and surreal. It became all the more surprising when the cause of death was revealed to be an overdose. Michael had apparently struggled with bipolar disorder his whole life, and during a recent manic episode had sought opioids, which turned out to be laced with fentanyl. Once the shock subsided, a feeling of betrayal set in.

As a soon-to-be therapist myself and a person living in the era of social media,

I understood the need for privacy. It wasn't that I would have expected Michael to announce his diagnosis to the public. It also wasn't that I'd expected him to be sober or above the desire to occasionally get high. It was that I'd believed he was above this kind of mistake. Only then did I realize I'd become attached to the idea that this man was superhuman. I realized I had needed to believe this because I needed to believe it was possible for me, or anyone, to transcend our human frailty. Even if I knew that I would never realistically attain such a level of immunity, I wanted to hold on to the hope that it was there as an option, should I ever be ready to pursue it.

As the stories poured in from Michael's students, I realized I wasn't alone in my feelings of betrayal. Others felt similarly shocked by the stark difference between their projection of who Michael was and the reality we were being forced to confront. The stories from those who knew him, however, were much different. They were the universal stories of people simply grieving. I realized that the man his family lost was not some inspiring idol, but a regular human. They were grieving a real person, some- one they'd known was struggling, who they'd wished they could have helped.

I felt ashamed of myself. In my attempts to replace reality with a fantasy where Michael was a hero, I'd separated him from the rest of us. How lonely he must have felt there, wanting to give people hope and also just wanting to be a creature on the earth. In Buddhism, there's a saying attributed to ninth-century monk Linji Yixuan: "If you meet the Buddha on the road, kill him." This is understood to mean that as we journey toward enlightenment, we'll encounter people who seem to have the answers. We'll want to idolize them, but we must be wary of this impulse. We must kill the fantasy we create in our minds that makes us believe it's possible to escape the chaos of life. Realizing I had made such a common error in projecting perfection onto this man was as humbling a lesson as the recognition that he was real.

My grandma was already ill by the time Michael died. I spent that day with her at the hospital, stunned and mostly dissociative. She could tell something was wrong but was too sick to pry. I was also in the final stretch of my graduate program and would need to return to Boston soon to finish my internship where I worked with clients who were often on the brink of hospitalization themselves. As her condition worsened, I made several trips back, each time finding myself more terrified by her worsening state.

I could see that she was dying, and I was embarrassed by my own inability to accept it. I understood the phases of grief, and was annoyed that my understanding didn't make me immune to denial. I watched myself act out this inner conflict in strange, immature ways, like lashing out at family members or even my grandma when I encountered tiny inconveniences. But each time fear or anger rose up, it was tamed by a slightly larger wave of love. My grandma's humanity was on such overt display that I found myself weak with care for her. The idea of doing anything but protecting her in her final days seemed out of the question. I surrendered to reality. Exactly three months after Michael died, I held my grandmother's hand in mine as she slipped out of her body. I sang to her as she went, and felt some delusion die then, too.

There's another teaching in Buddhism which says that every being has at one point been our mother. Through countless lifetimes and reincarnations, we have nursed from every breast and cried on every shoulder. This also implies that we, too, have mothered many. We have been the ones caring for those who are helpless, losing sleep so they could rest easy. The day my grandma died, I stood up straighter than I ever have. (I mean this metaphorically, as I spent most of that day on the floor.) Something inside me realized I'd missed the point. The roles we occupy as students or teachers are always temporary. No one gets to be a child forever, being cared for by the world. We have to grow up and take care of others. We have to hold our parents' hands and walk them back down the path they led us through. This is painful because it not only means saying goodbye to those that we rely on, but because it means no one is coming to save us. We have to take turns saving each other.

Despite my rocky beginning, I took to the role of therapist. At first, I found myself oscillating between total confidence and bewilderment daily, wondering what the job I had taken actually entailed.

"If we still struggle with the same issues our clients have, what makes us qualified to be their therapist?" I asked my supervisor one afternoon. She smiled like she'd been waiting for the question.

"I've been doing this job a long time, Chelsea. I had a new client once who came in for an intake, and as she started telling me these horrible stories about what she'd lived through and what her symptoms were like, I thought to myself, Wow, you really need some professional help. It took me a second to remember that I was the help." We both burst out laughing.

"I bet you think that was a long time ago, don't you?" she asked coyly. I nodded. "It wasn't." I was surprised and then surprised that I was still surprised. Since then, it's started to seem like our experience engaging with the struggle is what qualifies us to help others more than the promise of a solution. If someone tries to act like they have it all figured out, that now strikes me as the real red flag.

This world has no utopia. None, not one. Even once we understand this, our hope that we'll find out we're wrong comes back. Rather than trying to will that wish away, we can prune it gently and anticipate its return. We can greet it with kindness. The brave parts of us can offer the scared parts of us compassion. We may never find a perfect teacher and we may never be one, but we still have each other. And even if none of us know where we're going, so long as we take turns leading, we're still getting somewhere.

FUNERAL FOR WHO YOU USED TO BE

When you come out of the storm, you won't be
the same person who walked in.

—Haruki Murakami

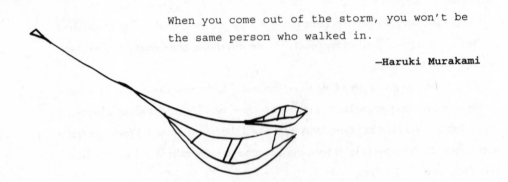

YESTERDAY, I GOT LUNCH WITH AN OLD FRIEND. THIS FRIEND AND I USED TO BE SUPER
close, like key-to-my-apartment close, cry-in-a-bathtub close, my-family-always-
asks-how-she's-doing close. But yesterday, as we sat across from each other, we
picked a lot at our plates. There were things we could say, but we weren't sure we were
still close enough to say them. Looking at her, I realized we didn't know each other
anymore. It wasn't that any horrible thing had happened between us. More that a
couple misunderstandings turned into a couple tense texts, which turned into a couple months without hanging out, which turned into an awkwardness even asking each
other when we might hang out again. Then a bunch of people died, we both got busy,
and, well, you know the rest.

I genuinely missed what we'd had. I felt sincerely sad observing the discomfort we'd
both hoped we wouldn't feel when we finally got together. But it seemed impossible
to deny. If we wanted to keep our friendship alive, we'd have to basically start over.

After I left, I scrolled through some old pictures of us. They were sweet photos, and I still treasure them. But none of the people in them seem to be me. That lady with the weird bangs she gave herself? Don't know her. The chick laughing hysterically wearing the same shirt I wore yesterday? Who is she? I could sort of remember how it had felt to take those selfies with my old friend, but mostly it seemed like part of a movie I'd watched while falling asleep. I realized I'm just not the same person I used to be.

Anyone who's been through a major transition knows the feeling I'm talking about. In times of great change, even the person we were two weeks ago can feel like somebody we don't know (and we're not sure we want to know). There are times when it seems like life will be boring forever, whole eras when nothing seems to change. Then there are times when every domain of our lives get blown apart. We get fired or evicted or both. We get sick or injured. Our relationships end or transform. We become morning people. Things we thought couldn't or wouldn't ever change now become suddenly unrecognizable. Cling as we might to what's familiar, at some point we're forced to let our old life die, and often the person we used to be dies with it.

In the words of writer Lidia Yuknavich, humans can reinvent ourselves endlessly. I believe we can die while alive. And I think we can truly start over. It takes courage to walk through that door to the total unknown of what can be, but it's sometimes the only real choice that we have.

A Funeral for Who You Used to Be is a way to celebrate this passage. It's a chance to thank the person you've been for getting you here, to this moment. It's a chance to dress up fancy and tell old stories. To listen to old music, and gently but firmly let others know that you're different now, that they have to get to know you again. Here's how to host one.

WHO

Deciding who to invite to your funeral is a strange mental exercise. But remember, this isn't a funeral for you, it's a funeral for who you used to be. The Old You, if you will. Try to imagine who that person would want there. Who were they friends with? Who were their crushes, their frenemies? Even if you haven't spoken to someone in years, invite them if you feel like Old You would want them there. What's the worst they can say? "This is really disturbing, please don't contact me again"? Sure, they could say that. But if they do, so what? They're friends with Old You, anyway. That person is dead. It's not hurting their feelings.

Here's an invitation template. Feel free to use or edit it as you see fit:

Hello, friends!

As you may know, I've been going through a lot of changes recently. I've realized that I'm not really the person I used to be, the person you knew. That person is gone, and I've decided they deserve a funeral. I hope you'll come celebrate their life with me!

As this is a funeral, we request formal funeral attire. Feel free to bring a story to share, an old photo for the memory board, or an object of significance to place on the altar.

WHEN

My funeral preference is Saturday afternoons, 1:00 p.m. to 4:00 p.m. People can come and go as they're able. If you're having lots of fun, you can go out for dinner and drinks afterward. You may also want to choose a date of significance—the date of a divorce, or the anniversary of an important event like a surgery or retirement.

WHERE

Your home, your friend's home, your childhood home—these are all good options. If those aren't available, ask if there's a community room in your apartment building, or at your local dance hall. Even your church will work, if they don't ask too many questions.

HOW

Decorate the room with things Old You liked. Make a playlist of their favorite music. Stock the snack bar with their favorite foods. Create an altar space for folks to add photos and objects of significance. Borrow or buy a dry-erase board, chalkboard, or corkboard so guests can leave personal notes. If you're able, place dark flowers at each centerpiece and dim the lights. Depending on the size of your group, you'll want to have a microphone and speakers ready to go. You may also want to prepare a projector for the photo slideshow.

Below is a sample itinerary. You can customize it to meet your needs, or to reflect the personality of the Old You.

1:00 p.m. to 2:00 p.m.: *Greetings, snacks, drinks*

During this time, invite guests to add to the message board where they can write a message to the Old You. (At 1:50 p.m., announce that it's time for guests to find their seats.)

2:00 p.m. to 2:45 p.m.: *Toast and roast*

Invite close friends and family to give a toast to the Old You. These can be as sentimental or irreverent as folks would like them to be. Finish with a speech that present-day you gives about the Old You.

2:45 p.m. to 3:00.p.m.: *Refreshment break*

3:00 p.m. to 4:00 p.m.: *Music and mingle*

Turn on a slideshow of photos of Old You's best and worst looks. Turn your playlist back on and invite guests to dance or mingle or share fun memories.

THINK ABOUT THE PERSON YOU USED TO BE.

WHAT MEMORIES OF THAT VERSION OF YOURSELF WILL YOU CHERISH?

WHAT DID YOU LOVE (AND FIND ANNOYING) ABOUT THEM?

WHAT WILL YOU MISS ABOUT THEM?

WHAT DID THEY TEACH YOU?

WHAT DOES THE NEW YOU KNOW THAT YOU WISH YOU COULD TELL THE OLD YOU?

A NOTE ON MOURNING WHO YOU COULD HAVE BEEN

When I hear people talk about grieving the person they used to be, I often hear a quieter hurt under that pain that's harder to articulate. I've come to understand this as the pain of mourning who we thought we could have been.

Many of us have traumatic histories, and we often assume we'd be living entirely different lives had we not been hurt so much. This pain is tricky to identify because it's an ambiguous loss. We can't really know who we could have become had our lives been easier. Many of us imagine there's some intrinsic, untouched version of ourselves buried under our injuries, a self that got stamped out by our struggles. We may even think that, with enough therapy, we can recover that person. In some ways that might be true, but it's more accurate to assume that we actually become who we are by existing within the conditions of our lives and by making choices in the face of our setbacks.

At some point, it becomes impossible to distinguish between our baggage and our personality. Maybe we'd have turned out different had we been better loved; maybe we'd be exactly the same (or even more messed up). What we really need to grieve is that we can never know. Because this pain is more private and personal, I don't advise hosting a party to grieve it. I do, however, encourage people with this grief to do inner-child work with a trauma-informed therapist, and also to place a photo of themselves as a child on their altar space, preferably next to a plant or a flower. Regardless of who you could have been, be proud of who you are.

FOREST BATHING

GROWING UP, I WAS NOT OUTDOORSY. I WAS THREE WHEN WE MOVED FROM RURAL TEXAS
to Nebraska, and while Omaha is no metropolis, it's more of a city than most realize.
The only parks near our house were tiny and mostly concrete. While I didn't have
anything against nature, I didn't really feel comfortable in it. I'm part of the generation
that first had personal computers, which became popular when I was in grade school.
These things were addictive right from the start. I didn't see the point in sitting outside
doing "nothing" when I could be on my computer recruiting strangers in AOL chat
rooms to sign up for my *NSYNC newsletter.

When I did go outside, I felt nervous. If others weren't close by, I felt alone. In a
bad way. At that time, I didn't understand how alive everything around me was. If I did
recognize the presence of wildlife, I assumed it was dangerous. Sadder still, I believed
I wasn't the kind of person who had a right to enjoy the outdoors. I could rarely afford
the gear, I couldn't really read a map, and I was a Girl Scout for only two weeks before
quitting. It seemed like hiking and camping were for rich people who had happy families and fancy tents and didn't quit the Girl Scouts.

Like most of my interests, pain is what finally drove me into the Great Outdoors.
I was an overworked grad student in Boston, had just gone through the most painful breakup of my life, and my grandma was getting sicker. I spent hours each week

driving around as an unpaid intern doing therapy with families in crisis. I needed my own therapist, but the waitlist at my university's counseling center was monthslong. I had recently made friends with some naturalists who were encouraging me to find remote spaces in which to rest and recover. I had tried going for walks in my neighborhood, but the streets were so packed that I felt like I was always in someone's way. At some point, I got desperate enough to search for somewhere more wild.

I drove my Kia Rio outside the city. I think I literally typed "woods" into my GPS and clicked on the nearest result. I wasn't dressed for the weather, let alone a hike, but I went anyway. I walked until I got tired, then plopped my butt down on a log and sat nodding at the hikers going by. There, I was greeted by an unfamiliar stillness. The quality of my thoughts started to shift. The trees seemed to be protecting me. I sat for a long time then went back again soon. The more often I did this, the better I felt. Despite the fact that I didn't have a special water bottle with a fancy straw or know any bird calls by heart, I began to feel at home in the woods. I'd sit for hours on the ground, eating a smashed protein bar from the bottom of my bag and dozing off. After a while, the people rushing by trying to squeeze in a workout on their lunch break seemed like the ones doing it wrong.

Having unlearned a lot of beliefs about nature, I see now how incorrect and concerning our collective attitude toward the nonhuman world is. I no longer believe there are nature people and nonnature people, I just think there are people who are more or less aware of their connection to nature. Humans are a part of nature. No matter how many cities we build, we can't separate ourselves from the earth because we're made of it.

We have come to think of ourselves as existing outside of the natural world in some separate realm. No one ever says this explicitly, but the idea is upheld through our behaviors, city structures, even our religious doctrines. We've developed the idea that we're fundamentally different from every other creature that exists, that we're more intelligent and sophisticated. To believe this is to misunderstand the earth and its dynamism. Every species experiences reality uniquely. Our planet is brimming with beings, many of which we haven't discovered and may never. Scientists estimate that more than 8.7 million species exist on this planet, and we've studied only about 1.2 million of them. Not only that, but we're constantly learning mind-boggling new information about the species we do know exist.

Woodpeckers have tongues so long they wrap around their brain to protect them from the force of their pecking. Dolphins have dialects based on what part of the ocean they're from. Bees communicate by dancing and sometimes take naps inside flowers. Elephants hold funerals for relatives and nonrelatives alike. The nonhuman world is full of its own feeling, ritual, and drama. Other creatures have societies, languages, and communities. Ecosystems are more complex and intelligent than we understand, and we're a part of that. By reclaiming our place in this vast web of life, we affirm that even our strange experiences are part of what it means to be an animal on earth.

Being immersed in nature is not just awe-inspiring, it offers a huge host of health benefits, which the modern medical industry is beginning to recognize. "Forest bathing" is a relatively recent term for a very ancient practice: walking in the woods. In 1982, Japan began issuing "green prescriptions" urging citizens to shinrin-yoku (or forest bathe) for their health. These days, many countries offer green prescriptions of some kind, and researchers keep discovering new benefits of going for a hike. Studies have found that just two hours of time spent in nature per week, all at once or in daily fifteen- to twenty-minute stretches, significantly increases self-reported levels of health and well-being. Forest bathing can also:

- *Regulate your pulse*
- *Lower your blood pressure*

- Lower your levels of cortisol, a primary stress hormone
- Strengthen your immune system (due to exposure to a diversity of microbes not found indoors)
- Increase your parasympathetic nervous system activity
- Reduce your risk of stress-based disorders
- Increase your focus and attention
- Boost your sense of meaning and vitality
- Reduce your feelings of depression
- Help you make new furry friends (please don't take them home)

If you don't have access to the woods or a national park, don't fret. In a pinch, even a bit of brush behind a Target will do. Just make sure you're not on private property and that your car isn't going to get towed.

The earth is always here. It knows things that were true long before we were born which will still be true long after we've returned to it, and it's ready to remind us of them. The planet moves on a slower timeline than our thoughts and feelings. Its rhythms are less frantic. Even still, the ground beneath us is active, alive, and constantly evolving. Just like our moods, the weather is continuously in motion. Nothing really stays the same for long. We can forget this if we sit in fluorescent rooms too much. Sometimes, an external reminder that fluctuations are healthy is all we need to feel stable.

When I lie down in the dirt and hear three birds call out to one another and feel an ant crawl on my hand and see the lichen growing on the bark, the story of my small life starts to dissolve and become a part of the myriad stories around me. The next time your feelings are too big, find a wild place. Sit down. Slow down. Drop any goals for as long as you can. The larger body of the earth will hold you. If you're tired of your own thoughts, listen to another chorus sing its song. The earth is teeming with life-forms old and new. Right now, a species we may never discover is being born. Life is sacred and full of possibility, and you, dear reader, are as much a part of that as any living thing.

WHAT IS YOUR RELATIONSHIP WITH NATURE? HOW HAS YOUR RELATIONSHIP WITH IT EVOLVED THROUGHOUT YOUR LIFE?

WHAT PERCEPTIONS DO YOU HOLD ABOUT WHO OUTDOOR ACTIVITIES ARE FOR? HOW DO YOU THINK YOU DEVELOPED THESE ATTITUDES? WHAT EXAMPLES WERE YOU SHOWN IN CHILDHOOD OF PEOPLE IN YOUR COMMUNITY SPENDING TIME OUTSIDE?

WHAT, IF ANYTHING, WOULD YOU LIKE TO CHANGE ABOUT THE WAY YOU RELATE TO NATURE NOW?

ARE THERE ANY WILD PLACES YOU'D LIKE TO DEVELOP A CONNECTION TO? HOW MIGHT YOU GO ABOUT DOING THAT?

THE WILL TO LIVE WALK

IN MY WORK, I OFTEN ENCOUNTER PEOPLE WHO ARE HAVING SUICIDAL THOUGHTS. This doesn't scare me. I was about ten when I first heard my mother say she wanted to die while in withdrawal. I was told that my paternal grandfather, whom I never met, took his life in a prison cell years before I was born. Years later, I stroked a dear friend's hair, wet from crying, as she lay in my lap and told me she couldn't keep going. I told her she could, but I was wrong. At her funeral, I hid under a flower display and tried to forgive myself for thinking I knew better than she did.

What I'm saying is that the will to live is not always available to us. Suicidal thoughts are common, but they are also serious. They are always an emergency. Sometimes, we get stuck inside a wound so big that we can't imagine an end to it. The absolute most important thing we can do in these moments is tell someone what we're feeling and push past any shame or fear until we get the help we need.

The research is clear: talking about suicide with someone does not increase their likelihood of self-harm. If anything, asking someone about their suicidal thoughts decreases the likelihood that they'll act on them. Still, the amount of stigma that exists around the subject of suicide is remarkable. If we want the suicide rate to go down, we need to normalize talking about it. Many of us have experienced thoughts like these.

It's one thing to feel hopeless, it's another to feel ashamed of feeling hopeless. We don't need to feel embarrassed. Suicidal thoughts are not a sign of weakness. They are simply a sign that we need help, and we need it right away.

If you're having thoughts about dying, please call someone right now. A therapist, a friend, a family member, a support group, a suicide hotline, or better yet all of the above. Just call. Say out loud the things you're thinking. That alone should give you some relief. Know that you matter. Regardless of who you are, you should not have to sit in this by yourself. And I know it might be hard to believe right now, but this feeling won't last forever. I can promise you that.

The next most important thing you can do is get some space from the thoughts and feelings you're having. My favorite way to do this is to go for a walk. Throughout the pandemic, I loved hearing people in quarantine talk about their "silly little walks" and how much they helped their mental health. Turns out, walks are pretty impactful. Research has found that walking offers many physical and mental benefits. It can also help us remember that the world is big, and whatever we're facing is not the only thing that's happening.

Walking is a form of bilateral stimulation. That's a fancy term for an activity that stimulates both sides of our body (and brain) in rhythm. The popular therapeutic treatment EMDR works in part by processing traumatic memories while engaging in bilateral stimulation. Its inventor, Dr. Francine Shapiro, actually invented the technique while on a mental health walk. By the end of the walk, she not only felt better, she'd invented a life-changing mode of therapy. Case in point. Bilateral stimulation helps us stop ruminating and encourages effective communication across various parts of the brain. This gives way to clarity and insight. It also reduces the intensity of an emotion by regulating our nervous system.

STOP DOOM SCROLLING
START DOOM STROLLING

WHO

Just you and all the creatures you'll encounter on your walk.

WHEN

Now? Or, the next time you're feeling trapped in your own head.

WHERE

If your neighborhood is quiet, walk there. Otherwise, the nearest public park, lake, woods, or any trail, really. Somewhere you feel safe.

HOW

There are many benefits to brisk walking for exercise, but that's not what we're here to do. Not right now, friends. It's time to slow down. I want you to walk awkwardly slow. I want you to walk suspiciously slow. I want you to walk "Mommy, why is that sad lady walking funny?" slow. I want you to stroll. Meander. In the tradition of Thoreau, I want you to saunter.

As you walk (and weird people out), look around. Take some long, deep breaths. Notice that the world is still here. Despite all the chaos inside you, the world is still here. Everyone is on their own personal pilgrimage. There are birds arguing with each other about dinner, trees holding decades of knowledge in a language we don't speak, seeds full of potential future forests being eaten by squirrels. There's probably a child screaming. None of this has to be here, but it is.

Notice how everything around you is fighting to exist. By allowing people to help you, you are doing this, too. Your desire to stop hurting is healthy. It's innocent. As you walk, notice the other creatures trying to get comfortable. Cats are chasing rats because they're hungry and rats are trying to get home without being eaten. The flower growing up through the concrete doesn't apologize for messing up someone's sidewalk. It wants to keep growing, and it's gonna do what it needs to do to make that happen. Be like that flower. Your desire to feel better is powerful, and it's natural. Simply by persisting, everything around you is expressing its will to live. That will still exists somewhere inside you.

Let memories of your life arise. Think about the things you've endured, the hardships you've overcome. I don't have to know you to know you've had to fight to survive. Life is like that. Thankfully, our bodies do a lot of the work for us. Feel your heart beating. The cells inside you are working tirelessly to keep you here. Even when you feel like you don't want to exist, they do. They want to live, and, in turn, they want you to live.

We will all die someday. Regardless of when or how, we'll pass through that mysterious vortex. Our stories will end. In the meantime, what else can you experience? What other version of yourself would you like to become? What feelings would you still like to feel while you're here?

WHAT HAVE YOU SURVIVED ALREADY? WHAT ARE YOU AMAZED THAT YOU'VE LIVED THROUGH?

WHAT THOUGHT OR FEELING IS MOST DIFFICULT FOR YOU TO HOLD RIGHT NOW? WHAT THOUGHT OR FEELING DO YOU WISH WOULD REPLACE IT?

IMAGINE THINKING AND FEELING THE WAY YOU WANT TO ABOUT YOURSELF AND LIFE. WHAT DO YOU BELIEVE WOULD CHANGE FOR YOU THEN? HOW WOULD YOU GO ABOUT YOUR DAY DIFFERENTLY?

FULL MOON FORGIVENESS PICNIC

WHEN THE MOON IS FULL, THERE'S A CERTAIN POTENCY IN THE AIR. THINGS FEEL MORE possible: revelations, reconciliations, release. Is there a simple scientific reason for this, like an increase of natural light in the environment? I don't know. More importantly, I don't care. I trust what I feel, especially when what I feel is enthusiasm for being alive. For those who follow the pagan calendar, the full moon is a time for letting go. The new moon is when we set intentions because everything is born in the dark. But when the moon is full, we marvel at the work that's already been done. We loosen our grip and practice surrender. This makes the full moon a great time for forgiveness.

Forgiveness is almost as magical as the moon. On the one hand, it's a universal task. We all have to practice forgiveness at some point. It's also extremely personal. It cannot and should not be forced. No one can tell us what or whom or when to forgive, and there are some things we may not forgive in this lifetime because the harm is just too big. That's okay. But before we make that call, we may want to reflect on what forgiveness is and what it's not.

Forgiveness is not about saying that what someone did was okay. It isn't a way of giving them permission to do it again. It's not a public endorsement or approval and it definitely isn't trust. Forgiveness is more like acceptance. Feeling able to accept that something happened is a sign that we have recovered. When we forgive, we stop denying the past. We acknowledge that harm has happened and affirm that we can go on. To forgive is to put down the burden of resisting our history. It is to stop trying to convince ourselves that things are better or different than they actually are. To forgive is to release ourselves from the grip of grievance and to accept reality as it is.

I have needed to forgive a lot of people in my life. I've forgiven my parents for not being present. I've forgiven other family members for being unable or unwilling to get sober. I've forgiven people from my hometown who took advantage of how easy a target I've been. I've also had to forgive myself many times, for being a real person, just as complex and fallible as everyone else I've forgiven. We will all need to forgive someone at some point, and we will also all need to ask for someone's forgiveness. This is inevitable, as there is no way to truly step outside of cycles of injury. Whether or not we're conscious of it, we all cause harm and will therefore all need to be forgiven.

Forgiveness isn't always a path to reconciliation. Sometimes I forgive someone and decide I never want to speak to them again. Sometimes that's the only way I can forgive them. These sentiments can coexist. There are times when forgiveness does mean giving someone another chance to be in our lives, and this can be a powerful choice. People mess up. Every single one of us has limitations. Giving someone the opportunity to learn and grow alongside us can be an extremely mature thing to do.

This next activity is designed for a time when you're ready to forgive someone. It may be a person who's still in your life, someone you've parted ways with whose past actions still affect you, or even yourself. It may be someone who's died or someone who doesn't even realize they hurt you. You may not know yet who you want to forgive, but you feel that there's some forgiving to be done. You may want to forgive the world for being such a difficult place in which to exist. Don't overthink it. Forgiveness may be a complicated subject, but picnics are not. You just sit down on the earth and eat stuff.

You can't fuck that up. The next time the moon is full and you're feeling forgiving, take yourself on a picnic.

WHO

I prefer this as a solo activity, but if you have one to three friends who are in the same forgiving mood, make it a small group gathering. I would not recommend inviting more people than that, because this activity is more introspective than others.

WHEN

Check your calendar for the next full moon, or the day on either side of the full moon. Preferably, plan to have your picnic at dusk so you can watch the moon rise. Night works, too, though. In fact, I love a midnight picnic. If possible, give yourself the whole evening. You'll enjoy yourself more if you don't have anything else to do for the rest of the night. Bonus points if you can sleep in the next day.

WHERE

You can have your picnic in a lot of places. Parks, backyards, cemeteries. Water is good for release, so being near an ocean or lake can be helpful. If the weather isn't great, a patio or sunroom can work so long as it has a view of the sky. It bums me out that we have to worry about getting shot or arrested for walking around in a field, but that's the situation, so be careful and make sure you're not on someone's private property.

WHAT

You'll need at least one cozy blanket, maybe two, and a pillow if you want to lie on the ground and look at the stars (recommended). You'll obviously need treats for the picnic portion, and there are tons of options on that front. My favorites are blackberries and blueberries, nuts (especially almonds and honey-roasted peanuts), goat cheese, olives, and red wine. A centerpiece of flowers is recommended, as is a bowl of dried herbs to burn. Tarot cards, your journal, and music are optional. If you bring candles, be careful not to start a forest fire.

HOW

Take your time setting out your goodies. Make your picnic decadent. Present it to yourself as you would to someone you'd been waiting a long time to see. If someone is with you, enjoy some long, luxurious silence together. Prepare yourself for letting go by slowing down enough to arrive where you are. Don't speak until you really have something to say.

Think of who you need to forgive. Remember the hopes you had for your relationship, how you felt before the harm happened. Honor the innocence of that trust and the innocence of any feelings of sadness or anger that arise. If it's yourself you're forgiving, try to recall the ideals you once held yourself to. Remember the feeling of wanting to be a certain person. Give that longing a moment of silence. A number of feelings may come up while you reflect, like grief, anger, fear, dread, even desperation. Notice whether you're still harboring any hope that things will change, or that you'll learn something which will reveal that things weren't as bad as they seemed. Whatever comes up, don't judge it. Just feel it. Hold it with care. See if you can notice the sensations the feeling brings up in your body.

I like to visualize the feelings I'm trying to release as a bundle of dead flowers, full of earthly matter that's ready to become something else. When you can sense the emotions in your body and/or have some idea of what they are, imagine yourself releasing them. Remember that you're not rejecting them or trying to destroy them. You're letting them go the same way you would scatter seeds or petals into the wind. You're allowing them to return to where they came from so you can do something else with that space inside yourself.

Sometimes, a grievance can be a way of staying connected to someone who is no longer safe to be connected to. If this is the case, forgiveness may bring up feelings of loss that you haven't previously been ready to feel. Be prepared for this possibility.

Treat yourself with extra tenderness if these feelings arise. Remember that everyone we have deeply connected with becomes a part of us, and we become a part of them. You are both forever changed because of your relationship, even now that it is over. Trust the mystery of how and when connections come into and leave your life. Trust that your future also holds mystery, and connections still to come.

As you feel these things leaving your body, give yourself time to sit with the now-empty space inside you. Notice what feelings or thoughts arise in response to letting this grievance go. Hold yourself with the kind of compassion you deserve and have always deserved, but which you haven't always received. Give yourself permission to let go and remember that the earth can hold whatever energy we release. The earth will always give us something fresh to fill these spaces with.

WHEN YOU THINK ABOUT FORGIVING, WHAT COMES UP?

ANY FEARS? BELIEFS? SENSATIONS IN YOUR BODY?

WHEN DID YOU FIRST WITNESS SOMEONE FORGIVING SOMEONE ELSE?

WHAT ASSOCIATIONS OR BELIEFS, IF ANY, DID THIS LEAD YOU TO HOLD ABOUT FORGIVENESS?

WHAT HAVE YOU LEARNED ABOUT FORGIVENESS SINCE THEN?

HOW MIGHT YOU HONOR THIS WOUND GOING FORWARD?

DO YOU NEED TO TAKE ANY ACTIONS OR COMMUNICATE ANYTHING TO ANYONE TO FULLY RELEASE THIS?

As you're winding down, feel free to speak these words to yourself or with those who accompanied you:

IN FORGIVING, I RELEASE

THIS OBSTRUCTION TO MY PEACE.

I AFFIRM THAT I SURVIVED

AND CAN MOVE FORWARD WITH MY LIFE.

WITH THANKS FOR THOSE WHO PROTECT ME

AND FOR THE GROUND BENEATH MY FEET,

I FORGIVE. I FORGIVE. I FORGIVE.

BLESSINGS IN EVERY DIRECTION.

INVISIBLE ARMY

You think your pain and your heartbreak are
unprecedented in the history of the world, but
then you read. It was books that taught me that
the things that tormented me most were the very
things that connected me with all the people
who were alive, who had ever been alive.

—James Baldwin

THERE'S A SPECIAL KIND OF SUFFERING RESERVED FOR PEOPLE WHOSE PAIN HAS NO NAME.
Those whose hardships have been so particular to their context that there aren't really
support groups for them or rallies being held on behalf of their issues. Pain itself is one
thing, but the loneliness of feeling like no one can relate to your pain is another. I've
always had unpopular issues, problems people couldn't quite understand.

As a kid, I didn't know a lot of others who had experienced the particular devas-
tation of being separated from a parent who was still alive, spending your life missing someone you never really knew and wondering if they were ever coming back. I
struggled with this feeling in part because I had no words for it. I hadn't yet found
language to describe my situation, so even I didn't understand it; I just knew I longed
for a connection that continuously evaded me. You know who did have words for that
feeling? Poets.

By my teenage years, I'd discovered poetry. I experienced a level of resonance and camaraderie while reading it that I'd never felt before. The writers I read had a way of taking my most complicated, confusing feelings and expressing them with beauty and brevity. It made things seem simple. Reading their words, I felt normal. Like my feelings made sense. Later, I realized that many of the writers I liked had led, well, pretty shitty lives. They, too, had felt like outcasts in their day. Concerned and annoyed by the plague of peculiarity that seemed to be haunting me, I did some research.

As it turns out, I wasn't the only one who'd been curious about the mental health of misfit poets. In 2001, two researchers studied the work of roughly three hundred poets from various eras and cultures, looking for linguistic differences between those who ultimately took their lives and those who didn't. The results were startling: those who died by suicide showed a markedly higher rate of individualistic language ("I") than less troubled poets, who tended to use words referring to the collective ("we"). In layman's terms, suicidal poets felt disconnected from others, whereas happier poets felt like part of a group. Ironic, seeing as how sad poets had been such a source of connection in my life.

After reading that, I committed myself to the task of feeling less alien. I realized that much of isolation is illusory—if these poets thought no one understood them while they were alive, and yet I felt totally understood by their feeling of not feeling understood (say that three times fast), then the likelihood that someone out there understands my feelings when I think they don't is also high. Furthermore, *nerd emoji* I realized that my sense of not belonging had been abated even without my discovering a physical community of people with my problems. I didn't actually need to know other outcasts in real life or be recognized by them to get the effects.

These people had mostly died before I was born, and yet I felt like they were somehow accompanying me through life. I thought about novels, how certain characters also made me feel less alone. I looked for more research and found that in 2011, researchers

A PITY PARTY IS STILL A PARTY

Shira Gabriel and Ariana Young conducted a study which found that reading fiction provided a sense of collective belonging to the groups described in the narrative. For superfans of any series, this might sound obvious, but I was amazed. Since then, I've incorporated this concept into my therapy practice (where I often work with self-identified misfits) and found that it works.

As I've continued living, I've discovered more ways that intangible figures can provide a sense of belonging when a physical community isn't available. For some, it's a connection to a loved one who's passed on. For others, it's a spiritual tie to ancestors they never got to meet. For those whose bloodlines don't provide belonging, there are movement ancestors who faced similar prejudice in the past and whose activism they feel indebted to. It can be nature-based and nonhuman guides. There are so many ways to feel connected. No matter how much it seems like it, we're never the only ones who have experienced something. Our pain is always only our own, and also never ours alone.

Here's how to connect with your Invisible Army:

- *Take some time to reflect. Ask yourself, who is my we? What ancestors, historical figures, fictional characters understand exactly what you're going through?*
- *Then consider: what does it feel like to imagine standing in front of this army of survivors who want to support you? What does it feel like to imagine not carrying this burden alone?*
- *Write them a letter. If possible, do it on real paper so you can hold it in your hands. Tell them what life has been like for you. Describe your struggles and moments of triumph. Make inside jokes. Thank them for the work they did in their lifetime to pave the way for you and help you feel less alone. Ask them for their advice going forward*
- *When you're done, fold it up and burn it to send it to the heavens. Bury it so it can become a future flower. Place it in a secret hiding place so you can read it later.*

BLESS THIS MESS

MAMA, IT'S BEEN FOUR YEARS AND SIX MONTHS WITHOUT YOU. AT LEAST, THAT'S what the calendar says. I'd clock it at more like eight or nine years in pain time, especially judging by the way I'm wearing the wreckage. People see pictures of me from four years ago and ask, "That's you?" I'm trying to find a way to feel proud of the impact my body has absorbed, but I'm not there yet.

You wouldn't believe the things that have happened since you died. Actually, you probably would. You know how life is. The humans are still hurting, no surprise there. Sometimes I feel like I'm clinging to a child-sized floatie in a tsunami. I wake up and have no idea what to do next. I try to dress myself, and it's like I've never done that before. Other times, like this morning, I feel that I can look life right in the face, that I can handle whatever happens. The earth seems to overflow with refuge. There's a breeze coming in that smells like clover, your favorite. Ripe peaches on the counter for sharing. I dip the toast in the coffee the way you taught me. It's a strange, silly world, and I believe I belong to it. I am strange and silly, too.

There are moments when I can't help but pray, though I don't know who or what I'm praying to. I don't really care. I feel like I could walk down the street and be destroyed by the silent heartbreak of just the people going by. It's like I can hear their most private, embarrassing dreams, which are usually about how much they want to pierce through their solitude and be known. I wish I could go around blessing them like a punk rock fairy godmother. I'd bless the cat lapping water from a dirty puddle. Bless the child translating directions for his mother. Bless the people working in landfills where one diaper will be decomposing for the next five hundred years. I'd bless the mushrooms and the vultures feeding on what we call trash, bless the ants carrying crumbs from our picnic back to their underground city, bless the truck stop diner where I waited for the storm to pass. Bless each one of us. Bless this mess.

I know there's cruelty everywhere, but when I sink into a bath after a desperately long day, I see kindness everywhere, too. I see the symbols carved into the faucet to remind me how to make the water hot or cold. I lather the soap and think of the people who made it, how they probably care whether I like the way it smells. I do. I think about the time I got lice and you spent hours combing through my hair to pick each egg out. You put on relaxing music, and I fell asleep. I wished I could have been your mama, too. I used to burn with the urge to protect you. I wanted to build a force field around you so you'd be safe forever, but then I'd realize how much I would hate to be trapped in a force field. Nobody wants that. The Talking Heads said heaven is a place where nothing ever happens. People want the chance to get hurt, which is to say, to live.

Last night I held a heartbroken friend in my arms as she cried. The neighbors were having a party, and their drunken laughter shook the windows. I considered walking next door to join them, and imagined the free food and drinks, plus the swimming pool. It had been a hot day. Then my friend shifted in my arms to get more comfortable, and I realized there was nowhere else to be. I sang to her and she wrapped her hand around my finger like a baby. You should have seen it. As the music got louder, she fell asleep.

I sat there thinking about pain, how it's a riddle, and how life so rarely offers an answer. I thought about how much we don't know and can't ever know, and how grateful I am to know that. I thought about the Rilke book you gave me that said to live the questions themselves, and how easily joy comes when we can. I thought about the time I made you that pendant out of clay when I was five. I scrawled my name into it in huge letters, as if you might otherwise forget who the artist was. Too cumbersome to be a necklace, I tied it up with excessive amounts of yarn and presented it to you with total confidence, knowing you would treasure it.

A few days later, we were walking down the street when we ran into some kids jumping rope. I'd never done that, so you stopped to show me how. You looked so proud, laughing and jumping in that driveway. But as your massive new necklace flopped up and down, the yarn started to break. Before you could grab it, the pendant hit the ground and split. I remember that I wasn't really sad that it was broken. I was sad because I saw how much you wished you could keep me from hurting, and your sadness in knowing you could not. Together, with your hand on my back, we gathered what was left and glued it back to one, but by then you were too scared to wear it.

Mama, we can't protect the people we love. Not really. We can only love them, and in doing so prepare them to live in a world that's often less than loving. Riddles and yarn keep us tethered here, clinging to this same heavy pendant of a life, at times barely hanging on. Even when I don't know basic things like where I am or what I'm doing, I know who I am because somebody knew me and loved me, lice eggs and all. Somehow, that's always enough.

ACKNOWLEDGMENTS

FUN FACT: DID YOU KNOW THAT BOOKS ARE NEVER ACTUALLY FINISHED? THAT'S RIGHT. Editors simply confiscate them from writers who, left to their own devices, will keep writing until they go mad and eat the pages. In all seriousness, though, if Albert Einstein was right in saying creativity is hiding your sources, then writing a book is losing track of your sources. This process was confusing. As I eked out final draft material by compiling ideas I'd scribbled on crumpled receipts, in text messages, and within the margins of my planner, I found myself second-guessing how I even knew any of these things. Many of the lessons that inspired this text were taught to me by way of influences so embedded in my psychology that I'm not sure where their teachings begin and end. I've done my best to name them all here, but I'm painfully aware that this list is not complete.

I did a lot of research to prepare to write this. But if I'm honest with myself, I came to believe most of it through experience. Even more than the web of intellectual sources that informed my thesis, I owe the inspiration for this book to those who have given me their fierce care before and during the time of my writing it. In doing so, you have proven the possibility of what I'm advocating for. Thank you to everyone, listed or not, who bought me lunch, rubbed my shoulders, listened to me grapple and pace, walked me home, picked me up, iced my jaw, slept next to me, took me to urgent care, and let me love you back. I'm grateful to have seen your messes and shown you mine, to know now what your thoughts sound like, and to be part of your mark on the world.

To those who most literally helped birth this book and whose hands touched the pages: My agent, Jess Regel, for making me feel like I know what I'm doing and for somehow knowing when I need to be told to chill. My editor, Kirby Sandmeyer, for helping me feel like this was my book to write. Your disembodied voice asking "What does this mean?" has become a welcome addition to my inner dialogue. To my almost editor, Haley Swanson, for taking a risk on me and filling me with hope at the earliest stage of this journey. And to Michele Lent Hirsh for the introduction, the fake deadlines, and for talking with me till 3:00 in the morning the night that we met in Montana.

To the people who helped me figure out what I had to say in the first place: Janis Campbell, without whom none of my words would be said with conviction. Every book I write is for us. Raynee Harvey, the one who taught me how to bring people together, for scratching and having my back in so many (way way) ways. Erik Anker, my psychonaut copilot, for your endless interest in my thoughts, and for seeing me (and us) as world class from the beginning. Valerie Kronberg, my best test subject, for making my brain better by linking it with yours, and for a friendship that feels like a party in a science lab. Lauren Graeff, my peaknuckle, and Lorne to be wild, for being a dream research assistant. Logan Graeff, my brilliant Berry, for the late-night assignments on history and philosophy. Joelle Wellansa Sandfort, my spider ma'am, for laughing at the absurdity and teaching me to look closer. Jason Thomas, who cares about animal crackers, for not letting me quit. Els di Maria Sofia, wisdom sister, for the treasure of our mutual mirroring. And Jordan Elsberry, for the saudade, and for helping me believe something I wanted to believe, though I'm still not sure what.

My teachers, past and present, formal and informal, whose signature is hidden in all of my work: Susann Suprenant, for admitting that creation is violent. Jack Phillips, for the higher levels of confusion. Rick Smith, for showing me how to be fed by the hunger. Michael Stone, for correcting my misunderstandings about intimacy. Mama K, for reminding me that there is always something to celebrate. And Mary, for the lessons in grace I am still poring over.

To those who offered me refuge in one way or another in an era when I so desperately needed it: Roger L. Lewis, the cutest motherfucker I know, for being there. Tim Maides, my original sweet tart, for somehow never being scared of me. Michelle Chamandy, for your infectious joy and incredible generosity. Mabel Elle, for welcoming me to Montreal with such open arms. Janice, JP, Isaac, Felix, and Leo, for making me feel at home where I otherwise would not. April Faith-Slaker, for being the one who told me to write this book first. Matt Stewart, for not giving up on me at the Sydney or since. Maggie Weber and Josh Poe, for putting up with my pickle juice. Michael Hennings and Sam Wampler, for being some of my favorite people to be squished between. And Gerald Balzer, for never once suggesting that we weren't real family.

To those who supported me in other ways: Michelle Ellis, true blue badass of a friend, for your needed reminders. Floris Van Vugt, for your radical empathy, and the precision of your idea(r)s. Demi Kulper, for your tenacity, your sweetness, and your deep belief in people (me). Erin Kilbury, for helping me have faith in the value of my raw edges. Jess Kim, for the ten-minute memos and the sounds of whatever you're cooking. Mari and Richard, for the cuddling assistance. And everyone who assured me that this process would eventually end when I very much felt it would not. I'm so glad it's over, and I can't wait to do it again.

BIG FEELS,

CHELS

NOTES

INTRODUCTION

xxi Gloria Steinem once: S. Benjamin, "No Slowdown for Gloria Steinem," CBS News, January 2006, https://www.cbsnews.com/news/no-slowdown-for-gloria-steinem/.

THE STRUGGLE IS REAL

8 how those genes are expressed: Center for Substance Abuse Treatment. (2014). Understanding the Impact of Trauma. *Trauma-Informed Care in Behavioral Health Services.* Substance Abuse and Mental Health Services Administration. Chapter 3. https://www.ncbi.nlm.nih.gov/books/NBK207191/; Mental Health America. Racism and Mental Health. https://www.mhanational.org/racism-and-mental-health; Torjesen I. (2019). Childhood trauma doubles risk of mental health conditions. *BMJ.* 364.

10 the social conditions we live in: M. Solan, "Health and Happiness Go Hand in Hand," *Harvard Health Publishing, Mind & Mood* (November 2021), https://www.health.harvard.edu/mind-and-mood /health-and-happiness-go-hand-in-hand#:~:text=The%20Harvard%20study%20led%20by,Waldinger; L. I. Pearlin, S. Schieman, E. M. Fazio, and S. C. Meersman, "Stress, Health, and the Life Course: Some Conceptual Perspectives, *Journal of Health and Social Behavior* 46, no. 2 (2005), 205–19, https://doi .org/10.1177/002214650504600206.

10 Violence is certainly not new: W. Koehrsen, *Has Global Violence Declined? A Look at the Data* (blog), January 2019, https://towardsdatascience.com/has-global-violence-declined-a-look-at-the -data-5af708f47fba.

10 Consistent intake of negative news: R. R. Thompson, E. A. Holman, R. C. Silver, "Media Coverage, Forecasted Posttraumatic Stress Symptoms and Psychological Responses Before and After an Approaching Hurricane," *JAMA Network Open* 2, no. 1 (2019): e186228, doi:10.1001 /jamanetworkopen.2018.6228.

10   Boston Marathon bombings: E. A. Holman, D. R. Garfin, and R. C. Silver, "Media's Role in Broadcasting Acute Stress Following the Boston Marathon Bombings," *Proceedings of the National Academy of Sciences*, 111, no. 1 (2019): 93–98.

10   74 GB of data a day: S. Heim and A. Keil, "Too Much Information, Too Little Time: How the Brain Separates Important from Unimportant Things in Our Fast-Paced Media World," *Young Minds* (2017), doi: 10.3389/frym.2017.00023

12   calories we consume: B. C. Ampel, M. Muraven, and E. C. McNay, "Mental Work Requires Physical Energy: Self-Control Is Neither Exception Nor Exceptional," *Frontiers in Psychology* 9, no. 1005 (2018), https://doi.org/10.3389/fpsyg.2018.01005.

12   a thigh does while running a marathon: P. Hochachka, *Muscles as Molecular and Metabolic Machines* (CRC Press, 1994).

12   burnout is a very real problem: P. Koutsimani, A. Montgomery, E. Masoura, and E. Panagopoulou, "Burnout and cognitive performance," *International Journal of Environmental Research and Public Health* 18, no. 4 (2021): 2145, https://doi.org/10.3390/ijerph18042145; N. Feuerhahn, C. Stamov-Roßnagel, M. Wolfram, S. Bellingrath, and B. M. Kudielka, "Emotional Exhaustion and Cognitive Performance in Apparently Healthy Teachers: A Longitudinal Multi-Source Study," *Stress and Health: Journal of the International Society for the Investigation of Stress* 29, no. 4 (2013): 297–306, https://doi.org/10.1002 /smi.2467.

12   compassion fatigue: *Merriam-Webster's Collegiate Dictionary*, 10th ed., Merriam-Webster Incorporated, 1999, https://www.merriam-webster.com/dictionary/compassion%20fatigue.

13   instances when one would normally care: C. Maslach and M. P. Leiter, "Understanding the Burnout Experience: Recent Research and Its Implications for Psychiatry," *World Psychiatry: Official Journal of the World Psychiatric Association* 15, no. 2 (2016): 103–11, https://doi.org/10.1002/wps.20311.

13   in life we can really count on: M. Solan, "Health and Happiness Go Hand in Hand," *Harvard Health Publishing, Mind & Mood*, (November 2021), https://www.health.harvard.edu/mind-and-mood /health-and-happiness-go-hand-in-hand.

14   Loneliness is a significant predictor: J. Yanguas, S. Pinazo-Henandis, and F. J. Tarazona-Santabalbina, "The Complexity of Loneliness, *Acta bio-medica: Atenei Parmensis* 89, no. 2 (2018): 302–14, https://doi.org/10.23750/abm.v89i2.7404; S. Buecker, M. Mund, S. Chwastek, M. Sostmann, and M. Luhmann, M. "Is Loneliness in Emerging Adults Increasing over Time? A Preregistered Cross -Temporal Meta-Analysis and Systematic Review," *Psychological Bulletin* 147, no. 8 (2021), 787–805 . https://doi.org/10.1037/bul0000332.

14   self-harming behaviors: A. Stravynski and R. Boyer, "Loneliness in Relation to Suicide Ideation and Parasuicide: A Population-Wide Study," *Suicide & Life-Threatening Behavior* 31, no. 1 (2001), 32–40, https://doi.org/10.1521/suli.31.1.32.21312.

14   reduces their intensity: E. A. Butler, B. Egloff, F. H. Wilhelm, N. C. Smith, E. A. Erickson, and J. J. Gross, "The Social Consequences of Expressive Suppression," *Emotion* 3, no. 1 (2003), 48–67, https://doi.org/10.1037/1528-3542.3.1.48

14   Self-regulation is important: K. D. Rosanbalm, and D. W. Murray, *Caregiver Co-Regulation Across Development: A Practice Brief* [OPRE Brief #2017-80]. Office of Planning, Research, and Evaluation, Administration for Children and Families, US Department of Health and Human Services (2017).

14   linked to dissociation: A. Schimmenti and V. Caretti, "Psychic Retreats or Psychic Pits? Unbearable States of Mind and Technological Addiction," *Psychoanalytic Psychology* 27, no. 2 (2010), 115–32, https://doi.org/10.1037/a0019414.

14   correlated to serious mental health issues: B. Goldman, "Researchers Pinpoint Brain Circuitry Underlying Dissociative Experiences," *Stanford Medicine News Center* (blog), September 2020, https://med.stanford.edu/news/all-news/2020/09/researchers-pinpoint-brain-circuitry-underlying-dissociation.html#.

14   chemical build-up can contribute: P. A. Levine, *In an Unspoken Voice: How the Body Releases Trauma and Restores Goodness* (North Atlantic Books, 2010).

15   benefits of time spent in nature: K. Weir, "Nurtured by Nature," *American Psychological Association* (2020), https://www.apa.org/monitor/2020/04/nurtured-nature.

15   ritual has been shown to dramatically: M. Lang, J. Krátký, and D. Xygalatas, "The Role of Ritual Behaviour in Anxiety Reduction: An Investigation of Marathi Religious Practices in Mauritius," *Philosophical Transactions of the Royal Society of London B, Biological Sciences* 375, no. 1805 (2020), 20190431. https://doi.org/10.1098/rstb.2019.0431.

15   social bonding, and emotional catharsis: N. M. Hobson, J. Schroeder, J. L. Risen, D. Xygalatas, and M. Inzlicht, "The Psychology of Rituals: An Integrative Review and Process-Based Framework," *Personality and Social Psychology Review* 22, no. 3 (2018): 260–84, https://doi.org/10.1177/1088868317734944.

THINKING STRAIGHT

19   one emotion roughly 90 percent of the time: D. Trampe, J. Quoidbach, and M. Taquet, "Emotions in Everyday Life," *PLOS One* 10, no. 12 (2015), https://doi.org/10.1371/journal.pone.0145450.

19   feelings to make good decisions: A. Bechara, H. Damasio, A. R. Damasio, and G. P. Lee, "Different Contributions of the Human Amygdala and Ventromedial Prefrontal Cortex to Decision-Making," *The Journal of Neuroscience: The Official Journal of the Society for Neuroscience* 19, no. 13 (1999), 5473–81, https://doi.org/10.1523/JNEUROSCI.19-13-05473.1999.

20   thoughts as more abstract or ephemeral: M. Solms, "Thinking and Feeling: What's the Difference?" *Future Learn* (blog), October 2015, https://www.futurelearn.com/info/blog/thinking-and-feeling-whats-the-difference.

20 The social implications of this idea: C. E. Izard, "Emotion Theory and Research: Highlights, Unanswered Questions, and Emerging Issues," *Annual Review of Psychology* 60 (2009): 1–25, https://doi.org/10.1146/annurev.psych.60.110707.163539.

REPRESSION CONFESSIONS

22 "stuck" in an emotion: E. Nagoski and A. Nagoski, *Burnout: The Secret to Unlocking the Stress Cycle* (Ballantine Books, 2019).

22 mortality across demographics: J. Giese-Davis, A. Conrad, B. Nouriani, and D. Spiegel, "Exploring Emotion-Regulation and Autonomic Physiology in Metastatic Breast Cancer Patients: Repression, Suppression, and Restraint of Hostility," *Personality and Individual Differences* 44, no. 1 (2008), 226–37, https://doi.org/10.1016/j.paid.2007.08.002; G. Maté, *When the Body Says No: The Cost of Hidden Stress* (A. A. Knopf Canada, 2003).

22 "Repression is actually a form of regulation": J. Suttie, "How to Become a Scientist of Your Own Emotions," *Greater Good Magazine* (blog), September 2019, https://greatergood.berkeley.edu/article/item/how_to_become_a_scientist_of_your_own_emotions.

22 "window of tolerance": F. M. Corrigan, J. J. Fisher, and D. J. Nutt, "Autonomic Dysregulation and the Window of Tolerance Model of the Effects of Complex Emotional Trauma," *Journal of Psychopharmacology* 25, no. 1 (2011): 17–25, https://doi.org/10.1177/0269881109354930.

CRY DIARY

28 award-winning actors: *Hollywood Reporter*, "Jennifer Lawrence, Brie Larson, Kate Winslet & More Actresses on THR's Roundtables," January 11, 2016, YouTube video, 1:04:42, https://www.youtube.com/watch?v=cBTvu66vc7g.

30 tearlessness occurs in roughly 7 percent: D. C. Hesdorffer, A. Vingerhoets, and M. R. Trimble, "Social and Psychological Consequences of Not Crying: Possible Associations with Psychopathology and Therapeutic Relevance," *CNS Spectrums* 23, no. 6 (2018), 414–22, https://doi.org/10.1017/S1092852917000141.

30 anxiety medications have been known: J. C. Holguín-Lew and V. Bell, "'When I Want to Cry I Can't': Inability to Cry Following SSRI Treatment," *Revista colombiana de psiquiatria* 42, no.4 (2013), 304–10, https://doi.org/10.1016/S0034-7450(13)70026-X.

30 Testosterone can decrease: L. Collier, "Why We Cry," *Monitor on Psychology* 45, no. 2 (June 2022), https://www.apa.org/monitor/2014/02/cry.

MIXED FEELINGS

33 mixed emotions are an indication: S. T. Charles, J. R. Piazza, and E. J. Urban, "Mixed Emotions Across Adulthood: When, Where, and Why?" *Current Opinion in Behavioral Sciences* 15 (2017): 58–61, https://doi.org/10.1016/j.cobeha.2017.05.007.

33 pleasure and pain is quite thin: S. Leknes and I. Tracey, "A Common Neurobiology for Pain and Pleasure," *Nature Reviews Neuroscience* 9, no. 4 (2008): 314–20, https://doi.org/10.1038/nrn2333.

33 a sense of meaning in life: R. Berrios, P. Totterdell, and S. Kellett, "When Feeling Mixed Can Be Meaningful: The Relation Between Mixed Emotions and Eudaimonic Well-Being," *Journal of Happiness Studies: An Interdisciplinary Forum on Subjective Well-Being* 19, no. 3 (2018), 841–61, https://doi .org/10.1007/s10902-017-9849-y.

33 increase in physical health factors: H. E. Hershfield, S. Scheibe, T. L. Sims, and L. L. Carstensen, "When Feeling Bad Can Be Good: Mixed Emotions Benefit Physical Health Across Adulthood," *Social Psychological and Personality Science* 4(1) (2013), 54–61, https://doi.org/10.1177/1948550612444616.

34 artists who have mixed feelings: F. Y. H. Kung and M. M. Chao, The Impact of Mixed Emotions on Creativity in Negotiation: An Interpersonal Perspective, *Frontiers in Psychology* 9 (2019), https://doi .org/10.3389/fpsyg.2018.02660.

REFINE YOUR PAIN PALATE

41 "name it to tame it" approach: Dalai Lama Center for Peace and Education. (2014). *Dan Siegel: Name It to Tame It* [Video]. YouTube. https://www.youtube.com/watch?v=ZcDLzppD4Jc

42 brain related to anxiety: M. D. Lieberman, N. I. Eisenberger, M. J. Crockett, S. M. Tom, J. H. Pfeifer, and B. M. Way, "Putting Feelings into Words: Affect Labeling Disrupts Amygdala Activity in Response to Affective Stimuli," *Psychological Science* 18, no. 5 (2007): 421–28, https://doi .org/10.1111/j.1467-9280.2007.01916.x.

42 state of the world in general: *Oxford English Dictionary* (n.d.), Oxford University Press, retrieved July 15, 2022.

43 lack of occupation or excitement: *Oxford English Dictionary* (n.d.), Oxford University Press, retrieved July 15, 2022.

43 ashamed or embarrassed: *Merriam-Webster's Collegiate Dictionary*, 10th ed., Merriam-Webster Incorporated (1999).

II. MESSY MINDFULNESS

45 A meditation practice has been shown: M. Thorpe and R. Link, "12 Science-Based Benefits of Meditation," *Healthline Nutrition* (blog), October 2020, https://www.healthline.com/nutrition/12-benefits-of-meditation.

47 estimated thirty thousand to seventy thousand a day: Neuroskeptic, "The 70,000 Thoughts Per Day Myth?" *Discover Magazine* (May 2012), https://www.discovermagazine.com/mind/the-70-000-thoughts-per-day-myth.

IN DEFENSE OF DEBBIE DOWNER

57 small talk are less satisfied: M. R. Mehl, S. Vazire, S. E. Holleran, and C. S. Clark, Eavesdropping on happiness: Well-being is related to having less small talk and more substantive "conversations." *Psychological Science, 21(4) (2010)*, 539–41. https://doi.org/10.1177/0956797610362675.

57 distress almost instantly: J. W. Pennebaker, *Opening Up: The Healing Power of Expressing Emotion* (Guilford Press, 1997).

57 suppressing their emotions as well as: B. J. Peters, N. C. Overall, and J. P. Jamieson, "Physiological and Cognitive Consequences of Suppressing and Expressing Emotion in Dyadic Interactions," *International Journal of Psychophysiology* 94, no. 1 (2014), 100–7, https://doi.org/10.1016/j.ijpsycho.2014.07.015.

57 Crying in the presence of a supportive: L. M. Bylsma, J. J. M. Vingerhoets, J. Rottenberg, "When Is Crying Cathartic? An International Study," *Journal of Social and Clinical Psychology* 27, no. 10 (2008), https://guilfordjournals.com/doi/10.1521/jscp.2008.27.10.1165.

58 Rent-A-Mourner: M. A. Mendoza, "Professional Mourners: An Ancient Tradition" (blog), *Psychology Today*, February 2018, https://www.psychologytoday.com/ca/blog/understanding-grief/201802/professional-mourners-ancient-tradition.

58 the well of human hurt can go: T. Mathew, "Professional Mourners' Lament from Quarantine," *The New Yorker*, June 2020, https://www.newyorker.com/culture/video-dept/professional-mourners-laments-from-quarantine; L. Lim, "Belly Dancing for the Dead: A Day with China's Top Mourner," *WYNC* (blog), 2018, https://www.wnyc.org/story/303342/.

LISTEN BUDDY

65 Active listeners: J. Zenger and J., Folkman, "What Great Listeners Actually Do," *Harvard Business Review*, July 2016, https://hbr.org/2016/07/what-great-listeners-actually-do.

65 The more we feel heard: V. K. Jahromi, S. S. Tabatabaee, Z. E. Abdar, and M. Rajabi, "Active Listening: The Key of Successful Communication in Hospital Managers," *Electronic Physician* 8, no. 3 (2018), 2123–28, https://doi.org/10.19082/2123.

65 to mimic theirs: G. J. Stephens, L. J. Silbert, and U. Hasson, "Speaker-Listener Neural Coupling Underlies Successful Communication," *Proceedings of the National Academy of Sciences* 107, no. 32 (2010), 14425–430, https://doi.org/10.1073/pnas.1008662107.

68 three specific forms of empathy: Key Step Media, "Different Kinds of Empathy" (January 2011), YouTube video, 4:53, https://www.youtube.com/watch?v=eg2pq4Mjeyo&t=35s.

70 shame makes us believe that we are bad: B. Brown, "Listening to Shame," March 16, 2012, TED Conferences, https://www.youtube.com/watch?v=psN1DORYYV0.

EVERYONE IS NEEDY

77 "low-maintenance person up close": B. Rogerson and S. Tatkin, "Attention and Presence," April 2017, in *The Therapy Spot*, audio podcast, 25:54, https://www.bethrogerson.com/stan-tatkin-security/.

77 people who have a secure attachment style: A. Levine and R. S. F. Heller, *Attached: The New Science of Adult Attachment and How It Can Help You Find—and Keep—Love* (Tarcher, 2011).

80 world from multiple perspectives.": S. B. Hrdy, *Mothers and Others: The Evolutionary Origins of Mutual Understanding* (Belknap Press, 2009).

81 oxytocin, dopamine, and serotonin: Eva Ritvo, "The Neuroscience of Giving" (blog), *Psychology Today*, April 2014, https://www.psychologytoday.com/ca/blog/vitality/201404/the-neuroscience-giving.

COULDN'T SELF-CARE LESS

92 $120 billion on self-care related to mental health: Global Wellness Institute, "Global Wellness Institute Finds Mental Wellness Is a $121 Billion Market," 2020, https://globalwellnessinstitute.org/press-room/press-releases/gwi-finds-mental-wellness-is-a-121-billion-market/.

92 assessing cause and effect: S. C. Thompson, "Illusions of Control: How We Overestimate Our Personal Influence," *Current Directions in Psychological Science* 8 no. 6 (1999): 187–90, http://www.jstor.org/stable/20182602; I. Yarritu, H. Matute, and M. A. Vadillo, "Illusion of Control: The Role of Personal Involvement," *Experimental Psychology* 61, no. 1 (2014), 38–47, https://doi.org/10.1027/1618-3169/a000225.

92 ourselves credit for it: R. H. Frank, "Why Luck Matters More Than You Might Think," *The Atlantic*, May 2016, https://www.theatlantic.com/magazine/archive/2016/05/why-luck-matters-more-than-you-might-think/476394/.

93 overemphasis on self-care backfires: F. R. Goodman, M. A. Larrazabal, J. T. West, and T. B. Kashdan, "Experiential Avoidance," in B. O. Olatunji (ed.), *The Cambridge Handbook of Anxiety and Related Disorders* (Cambridge University Press, 2019), 255–81, https://doi.org/10.1017/9781108140416.010.

NOT EVERYBODY'S CUP OF TEA PARTY

99 "the greatest barrier to belonging": B. Brown, *The Gifts of Imperfection* (Hazelden, 2010).

KNOW YOUR RITES

113 rituals are what make us human: M. J. Rossano, "How Ritual Made Us Human," in *Handbook of Cognitive Archaeology* (Routledge, 2018).

114 group of soldiers firing into the air": N. M. Hobson, J. Schroeder, J. L. Risen, D. Xygalatas, and M. Inzlicht, "The Psychology of Rituals: An Integrative Review and Process-Based Framework," *Personality and Social Psychology Review* 22, no. 3 (2018), 260–84, https://doi.org/10.1177/1088868317734944.

115 coping with uncertainty and failure: N. M. Hobson, D. Bonk, and M. Inzlicht, "Rituals Decrease the Neural Response to Performance Failure, *PeerJ* 5, e3363 (2017), https://doi.org/10.7717/peerj.3363.

115 Rituals also help alleviate anxiety: F. Gino, M. Norton, "Why Rituals Work," *Scientific American*, May 2013, https://www.scientificamerican.com/article/why-rituals-work/.

115 singing accuracy improved by 13 percent: A. W. Brooks, J. Schroeder, J. L. Risen, F. Gino, A. D. Galinsky, M. I. Norton, and M. E. Schweitzer, "Don't Stop Believing: Rituals Improve Performance by Decreasing Anxiety," *Organizational Behavior and Human Decision Processes* 137 (2016), 71–85, https://doi.org/10.1016/j.obhdp.2016.07.004.

115 rituals can induce a state known as "flow": M. Csikszentmihalyi, *Flow: The Psychology of Optimal Experience* (Harper&Row, 1990).

115 Flow can feel to some like a transcendent: S. Engeser, A. Schiepe-Tiska, C. Peifer, "Historical Lines and an Overview of Current Research on Flow," in C. Peifer and S. Engeser (eds.), *Advances in Flow Research* (Springer, 2021), https://doi.org/10.1007/978-3-030-53468-4_1.

115 bottom-up processing occurs: V. Rousay, "Bottom-Up Processing," *Simply Psychology*, January 2021, simplypsychology.org/bottom-up-processing.html.

116 group rituals are a powerful way to quickly and reliably: S. J. Charles, V. van Mulukom, J. E. Brown, F. Watts, R. Dunbar, and M. Farias, "United on Sunday: The Effects of Secular Rituals on Social Bonding and Affect," *PLOS One* 16, no. 1 (2021), e0242546, https://doi.org/10.1371/journal.pone.0242546; A. Markman, "Why Do People Engage in Extreme Rituals?" (blog), *Psychology Today*, September 2012, https://www.psychologytoday.com/us/blog/ulterior-motives/201309/why-do-people-engage-in-extreme-rituals.

116 we spend the most time with: K. Ibarrola, "Good Friends Mimic Each Other's Brainwaves, Neuroscientist Claims," Inquirer.net, Science, Health and Research (blog), November 2017, https://technology.inquirer.net/69088/good-friends-mimic-others-brainwaves-neuroscientist-claims.

116 firewalkers themselves with astonishing precision: D. Xygalatas, I. Konvalinka, J. Bulbulia, and
A. Roepstorff, "Quantifying Collective Effervescence: Heart-Rate Dynamics at a Fire-Walking Ritual,
Communicative & Integrative Biology 4, no. 6 (2011), 735–38, https://doi.org/10.4161/cib.17609.

116 Collective effervescence (CE for short) is experienced: Ibid.

116 feeling of transcendence that: "Émile Durkheim," *Internet Encyclopedia of Philosophy*, https://iep.
utm.edu/emile-durkheim/.

116 opportunity for transformation: W. H. Houff, *Infinity in Your Hand: A Guide for the Spiritually
Curious* (Skinner House Books, 1993).

117 clapping when they were told to stomp: K. Mills (host), "Speaking of Psychology: COVID-19
and the Loss of Rituals, Formation of New Ones," with Michael Norton, PhD, Episode 106, May 2020,
audio podcast, 22:24, https://www.apa.org/news/podcasts/speaking-of-psychology/ritual-loss-covid-19.

119 Environment greatly affects our mood: S. Liddicoat, "The Therapeutic Waiting Room: Therapist
and Service User Perspectives on the Psychologically Supportive Dimensions of Architectural Space,"
HERD: Health Environments Research & Design Journal, 13, no. 2 (2020): 103–18, https://doi
.org/10.1177/1937586720904805.

LOSE IT CREW

124 when two people are bonding: A. Carpenter, K. Greene, "Social Penetration Theory," in the *International
Encyclopedia of Interpersonal Communication* (2015), https://doiorg/10.1002/9781118540190.wbeic160;
I. Altman and D. A. Taylor, *Social Penetration: The Development of Interpersonal Relationships* (Holt,
Rinehart and Winston, 1973).

CUDDLE PUDDLE

147 including HIV and cancer: S. Kale, "Skin Hunger Helps Explain Your Desperate Longing for Human
Touch," *Wired*, April 2020, https://www.wired.co.uk/article/skin-hunger-coronavirus-human-touch.

147 Touch can help cure insomnia: F. Mancini, T. Nash, G. D. Iannetti, and P. Haggard, "Pain Relief
by Touch: A Quantitative Approach," *Pain* 155, no. 3 (2014), 635–42, https://doi.org/10.1016/j
.pain.2013.12.024.

147 when the touch comes from someone we love: J. A. Coan, H. S. Schaefer, and R. J. Davidson,
"Lending a Hand: Social Regulation of the Neural Response to Threat," *Psychological Science* 17, no. 12
(2006), 1032–39, https://doi.org/10.1111/j.1467-9280.2006.01832.x.

147 Bonnie and Clyde effect: C. K. De Dreu, "Oxytocin Modulates Cooperation Within and
Competition Between Groups: An Integrative Review and Research Agenda," *Hormones and Behavior*
61, no. 3 (2012), 419–28, https://doi.org/10.1016/j.yhbeh.2011.12.009; C. K. W. De Dreu, L. L. Greer,

G. A. Van Kleef, S. Shalvi, and M. J. J., "Oxytocin Promotes Human Ethnocentrism," *Proceedings of the National Academy of Sciences* 108, no. 4 (2011), 1262–66, https://doi.org/10.1073/pnas.1015316108.

TOWN CRIER CHOIR

153 Singing, especially in a community setting,: G. F. Welch, E. Himonides, J. Saunders, I. Papageorgi, and M. Sarazin, "Singing and Social Inclusion," *Frontiers in Psychology* 5, no. 803 (2014), https://doi.org/10.3389/fpsyg.2014.00803.

153 Some anthropologists believe that singing: D. Weinstein, J. Launay, E. Pearce, et al., "Singing and Social Bonding: Changes in Connectivity and Pain Threshold as a Function of Group Size," *Evolution and Human Behavior* 37, no. 2 (2016), 152–58, https://doi.org/10.1016/j.evolhumbehav.2015.10.002.

154 Singing also has physiological benefits: G. Kreutz, S. Bongard, S. Rohrmann, et al., "Effects of Choir Singing or Listening on Secretory Immunoglobulin A, Cortisol, and Emotional State," *Journal of Behavioral Medicine* 27, no. 6 (2004): 623–35, https://doi.org/10.1007/s10865-004-0006-9.

154 higher pain tolerance: R. I. M. Dunbar, K. Kaskatis, I. MacDonald, and V. Barra, "Performance of Music Elevates Pain Threshold and Positive Affect: Implications for the Evolutionary Function of Music," *Evolutionary Psychology* 10, no. 4 (2012): 688–702, https://doi.org/10.1177/147470491201000403.

154 Singing also improves oxygen levels: A. M. Idrose, N. Juliana, S. Azmani, et al., "Singing Improves Oxygen Saturation in Simulated High-Altitude Environment," *Journal of Voice* 36, no. 3 (2022), https://doi.org/10.1016/j.jvoice.2020.06.031.

154 enhances memory function: S. E. Osman, V. Tischler, and J. Schneider, "Singing for the Brain: A Qualitative Study Exploring the Health and Well-Being Benefits of Singing for People with Dementia and Their Careers," *Dementia* 15, no. 6 (2016), 1326–39, https://doi.org/10.1177/1471301214556291.

154 Singing with others helps us process grief: D. Fancourt, S. Finn, K. Warran, T. Wiseman, "Group Singing in Bereavement: Effects on Mental Health, Self-Efficacy, Self-Esteem and Well-Being," *BMJ Supportive & Palliative Care* 12, no. 4 (June 2019), doi: 10.1136/bmjspcare-2018-001642.

158 songs that are "word-rich" and "vowel-rich": B. Eno, "Singing: The Key to a Long Life," November 2008, in *Weekend Edition Sunday*, NPR, produced by Jay Allison and Dan Gediman, audio podcast, 5:29, https://www.npr.org/2008/11/23/97320958/singing-the-key-to-a-long-life.

DANCING WITH MYSELVES

159 3000 BC in Egypt, when dancing became: J. J. Mark, "Music & Dancing in Ancient Egypt," *World History Encyclopedia*, May 2017, https://www.worldhistory.org/article/1075/music—dance-in-ancient-egypt/.

161 dancing stimulates our brain's reward centers: J. Krakauer, "Why Do We Like to Dance—and Move to the Beat?," *Scientific American*, September 2008, https://www.scientificamerican.com/article/experts-dance/.

161 to make and set goals: A. R. Salo, "The Power of Dance: How Dance Affects the Mental and Emotional Health and Self-Confidence in Young Adults" (master's thesis, University of Northern Colorado, 2019), https://digscholarship.unco.edu/cgi/viewcontent.cgi?article=1192&context=theses.

161 reduces the risk of dementia: J. Verghese, R. B. Lipton, M. J. Katz, et al., "Leisure Activities and the Risk of Dementia in the Elderly," *New England Journal of Medicine* 348, no. 25 (2003): 2508–16, https://doi.org/10.1056/NEJMoa022252.

161 potentially traumatic circumstances: J. Leseho and L. R. Maxwell, "Coming Alive: Creative Movement as a Personal Coping Strategy on the Path to Healing and Growth," *British Journal of Guidance & Counselling* 38, no. 1 (2010): 17–30, https://doi.org/10.1080/03069880903411301.

ALL VIBES MATTER

168 as their white peers.: K. M. Hoffman, K. S. Trawalter, J. R. Axt, and M. N. Oliver, "Racial Bias in Pain Assessment and Treatment Recommendations, and False Beliefs About Biological Differences Between Blacks and Whites," *Proceedings of the National Academy of Sciences* 113, no. 16 (2016), https://doi.org/10.1073/pnas.1516047113.

168 by physicians in the 1800s: S. Trawalter, "Black Americans Are Systematically Under-Treated for Pain. Why?" (blog), Frank Batten School of Leadership and Public Policy, 2020, https://batten.virginia.edu/about/news/black-americans-are-systematically-under-treated-pain-why.

168 even more fragmented: L. Haskell and M. Randall, "The Impact of Trauma on Adult Sexual Assault Victims," *Justice Canada* (2019).

168 While men are less likely to be assaulted: "The Birds and the Bees NS. What Is Sexual Violence?" October 4, 2016, https://www.youtube.com/watch?v=S4G2ZOAu1pE. https://www.youtube.com/watch?v=S4G2ZOAu1pE.

168 affront to a man's dominance: J. Kuadli, "32 Shocking Sexual Assault Statistics for 2022," *Legaljobs* (blog), January 2021, https://legaljobs.io/blog/sexual-assault-statistics/.

168 We know that homophobia: Fenway Institute, National LGBT Health Education Center, "Suicide Risk and Prevention for LGBTQ People," (September 2018), https://www.lgbtqiahealtheducation.org/wp-content/uploads/2018/10/Suicide-Risk-and-Prevention-for-LGBTQ-Patients-Brief.pdf.

169 *Internalized homophobia: G. Wen and L. Zheng, "The Influence of Internalized Homophobia on Health-Related Quality of Life and Life Satisfaction Among Gay and Bisexual Men in China," American Journal of Men's Health 13, no. 4 (2019), https://doi.org/10.1177/1557988319864775.*

170   high levels of social privilege: G. A. van Kleef, C. Oveis, I. van der Löwe, et al., "Power, Distress, and Compassion: Turning a Blind Eye to the Suffering of Others," *Psychological Science* 19, no. 12 (2008), 1315–22, https://doi.org/10.1111/j.1467-9280.2008.02241.x.

170   lower socioeconomic status: M. W. Kraus, S. Côté, and D. Keltner, D, "Social Class, Contextualism, and Empathic Accuracy," *Psychological Science* 21, no. 11 (2010): 1716–1723, https://doi.org/10.1177/0956797610387613.

FUNERAL FOR WHO YOU USED TO BE

189   humans can reinvent ourselves endlessly: L. Yuknavitch, *The Beauty of Being a Misfit*. Filmed 2016. TED video, 12:49. https://www.ted.com/talks/lidia_yuknavitch_the_beauty_of_being_a_misfit?language=en.

FOREST BATHING

197   8.7 million different species exist on the planet: National Geographic Resource Library, Definition of Biodiversity, retrieved July 15, 2022.

197   two hours of time: M. P. White, I. Alcock, J. Grellier, et al., "Spending at Least 120 Minutes a Week in Nature Is Associated with Good Health and Wellbeing," *Scientific Reports* 9, no. 7730 (2019), https://doi.org/10.1038/s41598-019-44097-3.

198   Strengthen your immune system: G. Rook, "Regulation of the Immune System by Biodiversity from the Natural Environment: An Ecosystem Service Essential to Health," *Proceedings of the National Academy of Sciences* 110, no. 46 (2013), https://www.pnas.org/doi/10.1073/pnas.1313731110.

198   Reduce your risk of stress-based disorders: B. J. Park, Y. Tsunetsugu, T. Kasetani, et al., "The Physiological Effects of *Shinrin-yoku* (Taking in the Forest Atmosphere or Forest Bathing): Evidence from Field Experiments in 24 Forests Across Japan," *Environtal Health Preventive Medicine* 15, no. 18 (2010), https://doi.org/10.1007/s12199-009-0086-9.

198   Increase your focus and attention: M. M. Hansen, R. Jones, and K. Tocchini, "Shinrin-Yoku (Forest Bathing) and Nature Therapy: A State-of-the-Art Review. *International journal of environmental research and public health*, 14(8) (2017), 851. https://doi.org/10.3390/ijerph14080851.

198   Boost your sense of meaning and vitality: B. Oh, K. J. Lee, C. Zaslawski, A. Yeung, D. Rosenthal, L. Larkey, and M. Back, "Health and Well-Being Benefits of Spending Time in Forests: Systematic Review," *Environmental Health and Preventive Medicine* 22, no. 1 (2017): 71, https://doi.org/10.1186/s12199-017-0677-9.

198   Reduce your feelings of depression: A. Furuyashiki, K. Tabuchi, K., Norikoshi, T. Kobayashi, and S. Oriyama, "A Comparative Study of the Physiological and Psychological Effects of Forest Bathing

(Shinrin-yoku) on Working Age People with and Without Depressive Tendencies," *Environmental Health and Preventive Medicine* 24, no. 1 (2019): 46, https://doi.org/10.1186/s12199-019-0800-1.

THE WILL TO LIVE WALK

200 about their suicidal thoughts: T. Dazzi, R. Gribble, S. Wessely, and N. T. Fear, N. T. "Does Asking About Suicide and Related Behaviours Induce Suicidal Ideation? What Is the Evidence?" *Psychological Medicine* 44, no. 16 (2014): 3361–63, https://doi.org/10.1017/S0033291714001299.

201 physical and mental benefits.: M. Johansson, T. Hartig, and H. Staats, "Psychological Benefits of Walking: Moderation by Company and Outdoor Environment," *Applied Psychology: Health and Well -Being* 3 (2011), 261–80.

201 regulating our nervous system: A. Serin, N. S. Hageman, and E. Kade, "The Therapeutic Effect of Bilateral Alternating Stimulation Tactile Form Technology on the Stress Response," *Journal of Biotechnology and Biomedical Science* 1, no. 2 (2018): 42–47.

202 walking for exercise: M. Hamer and Y. Chida, "Walking and Primary Prevention: A Meta-Analysis of Prospective Cohort Studies," *British Journal of Sports Medicine* 42, no. 4 (2008): 238–43, https://doi.org/10.1136/bjsm.2007.039974.

INVISIBLE ARMY

214 *The results were startling: S. W. Stirman and J. W. Pennebaker, "Word Use in the Poetry of Suicidal and Nonsuicidal Poets," Psychosomatic Medicine 63, no. 4 (2001): 517–22. https://doi.org/10.1097/00006842-200107000-00001.*

214 *researchers Shira Gabriel and Ariana Young: S. Gabriel and A. F. Young, "Becoming a Vampire Without Being Bitten: The Narrative Collective-Assimilation Hypothesis," Psychological Science 22, no. 8 (2011): 990–94, http://www.jstor.org/stable/25835489.*

INDEX

avoiding shame spirals, *70*,
70–72
empathy and, 67–69
evaluating your listening skills,
69
hijacking the interaction, 71
how to listen well, 66–67
making mistakes in listening,
70
Lorde, Audre, 17, 99

M

MacDonald, George, 128
medical system, failures of,
90–91
meditation, 45–46
anywhere meditation
practice, instructions, 48
benefits of, 45, 46–47
ecstatic dance and, 160–61
mindfulness vs., 46
mental health, 8–10, 13, 18, 76,
90–91, 92, 169
benefits of ritual, 115
benefits of time spent in
nature, 15
burnout and, 12
as complex issue, 8
dissociation and, 14–15
increase in discussions about,
xv
loneliness and, 14
mindfulness for, 45–48
modern data diet and, 10–11
of poets, 213
psychotherapy for, xv–xvi

rates of mental illness, xv
ritual and, 115
social conditions and, 10
state of "flow" and, 115
walking for, 201–4
See also anxiety; depression;
healing; hypervigilance;
suicide/suicidal thoughts
#MeToo movement, 168
mindfulness, 45–48
anywhere meditation
practice, instructions, 48
benefits of, 47
identifying an emotion, 47
what it is, what it is not, 46
mixed feelings, 33–35
as bittersweet, 33, 34, 35
conflicted or confused, 33
creativity and, 34
happiness and, 33
mixed feelings we love, 35
pleasure and pain, 33, 35
questions to ask yourself, 35
Wheel of Emotions, *34*
"moment sauce," 119
mourning, 58–59
agony altar and, 51
in ancient times, 58
in China and England, 58
ecstatic dance and, 160–61
mourning who you could have
been, 193
professional (moirology), 58
ritual and, 115, 117
Murakami, Haruki, 188
music

author and, xviii
cry baby creed and, 3
cry playlist, 31
dance playlist, 162–63
for Funeral for Who You Used
to Be, 191, 192
group singing, 153–58
mixed feelings and, 35
processing feedback and, 103,
105
rituals and, 119

N

Nagoski, Amelia and Emily, 22
nature
being attuned to, 15
benefits of time spent in, 15,
197–98, 201
cycles and phases, 15
forest bathing, 195–99
Full Moon Forgiveness Picnic,
205–11
interesting facts, 197
number of species, 197
weather and, 198
The Will to Live Walk, 201–4
neediness/relational needs,
76–82
attachment style and, 77–81
list of common types, *82*, 82
questions to ask yourself, 82
reciprocal caregiving, 81
repression of, 77, 80
sickness and, 95–96, 98
as universal, 76–77
Norton, Michael, 117

ABOUT THE AUTHOR

CHELSEA HARVEY GARNER is a writer, psychotherapist, and director of Big Feels Lab, a nonprofit that promotes collective mental health. In her clinical practice, she specializes in helping misfits, survivors, and unconventional families reclaim a sense of dignity and connect with one another more deeply. When not working, she can be found starting dance parties in public and hosting cuddle puddles at her home in NYC.